This Book Belongs To

....

Coloring Tips

\# Sometimes what you think the color will look like and what it will actually look like are very different. Use the color test page.

\# Don't press too hard. Start out coloring lightly and you can always go back and make it darker.

\# Keep your pencil tips sharp so you can get into all the intricate spaces.

\# Using markers? Place a scrap piece of paper behind the page you are coloring. Pages in this book are only printed on one side but there is still the risk of bleed through to the next page.

\# Try different coloring utensils marketed for adults. It is fun and quality can vary greatly.

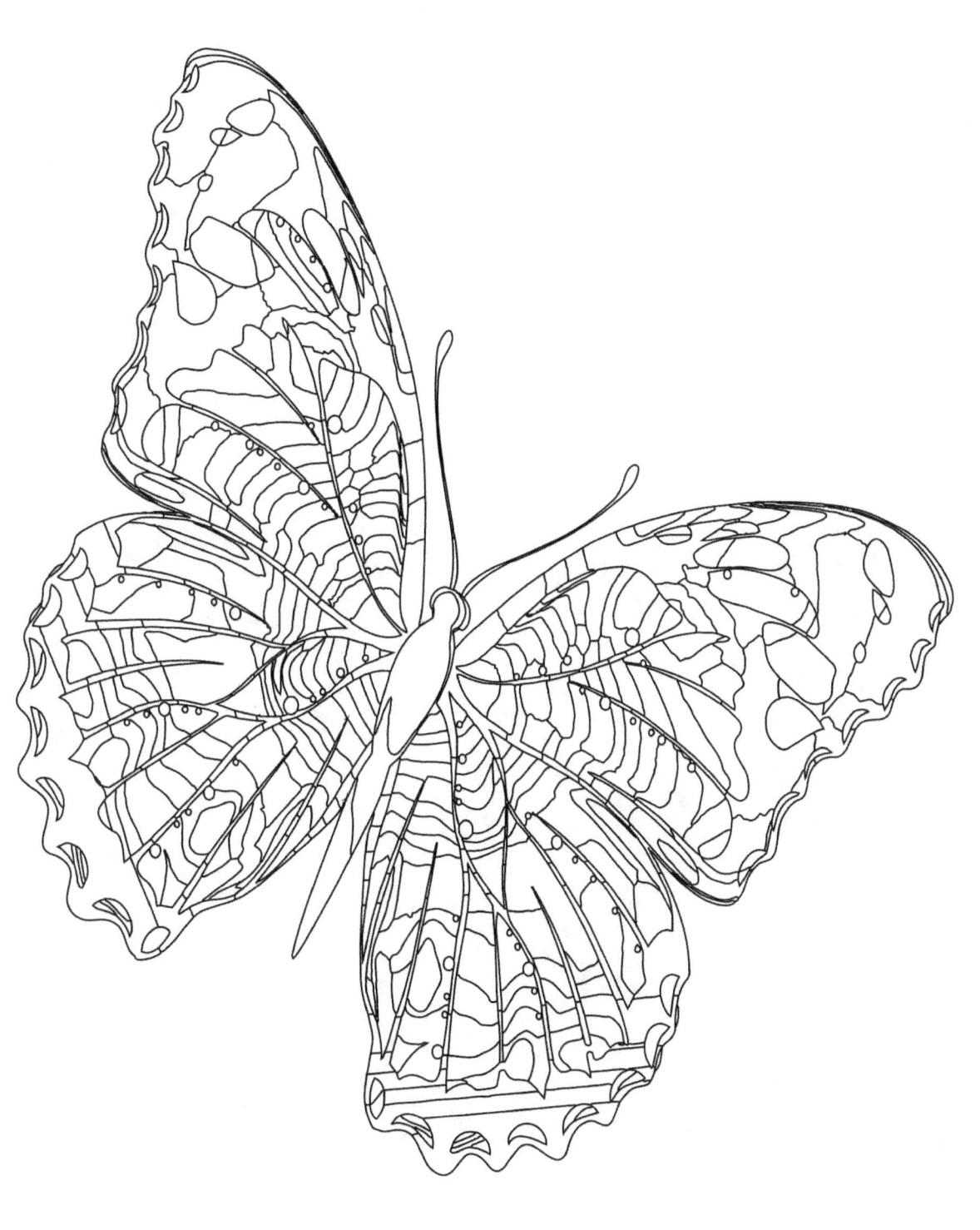

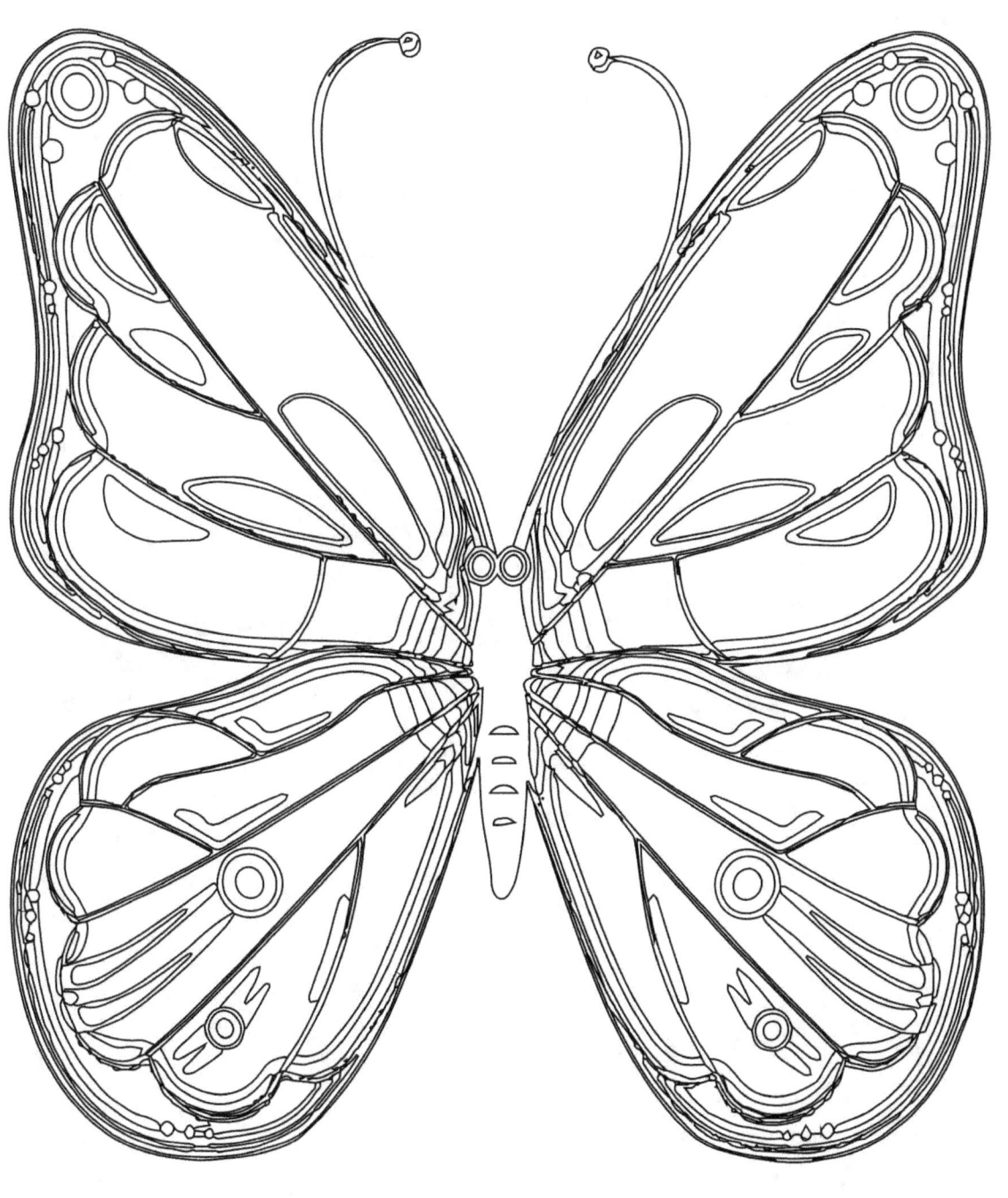

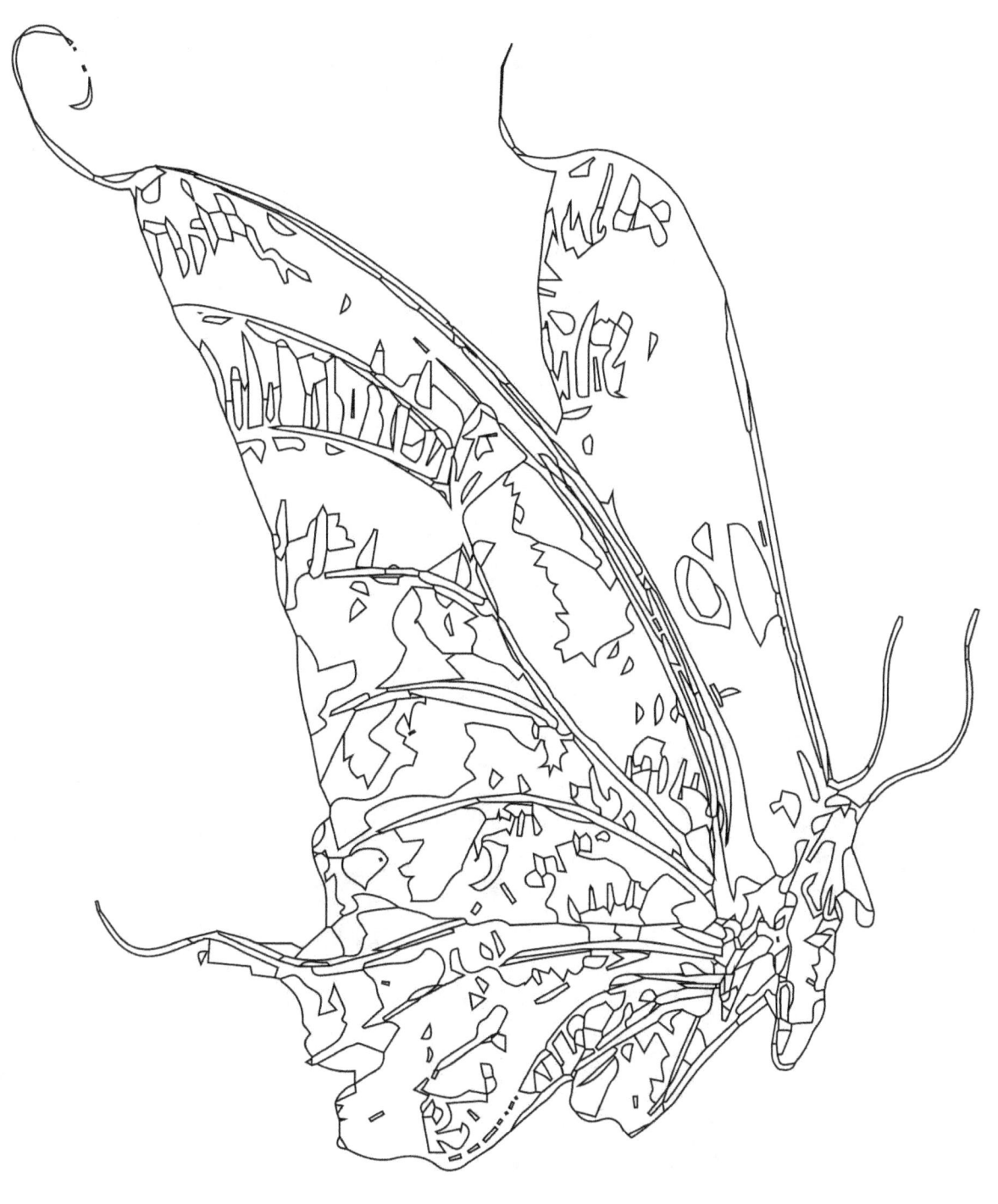

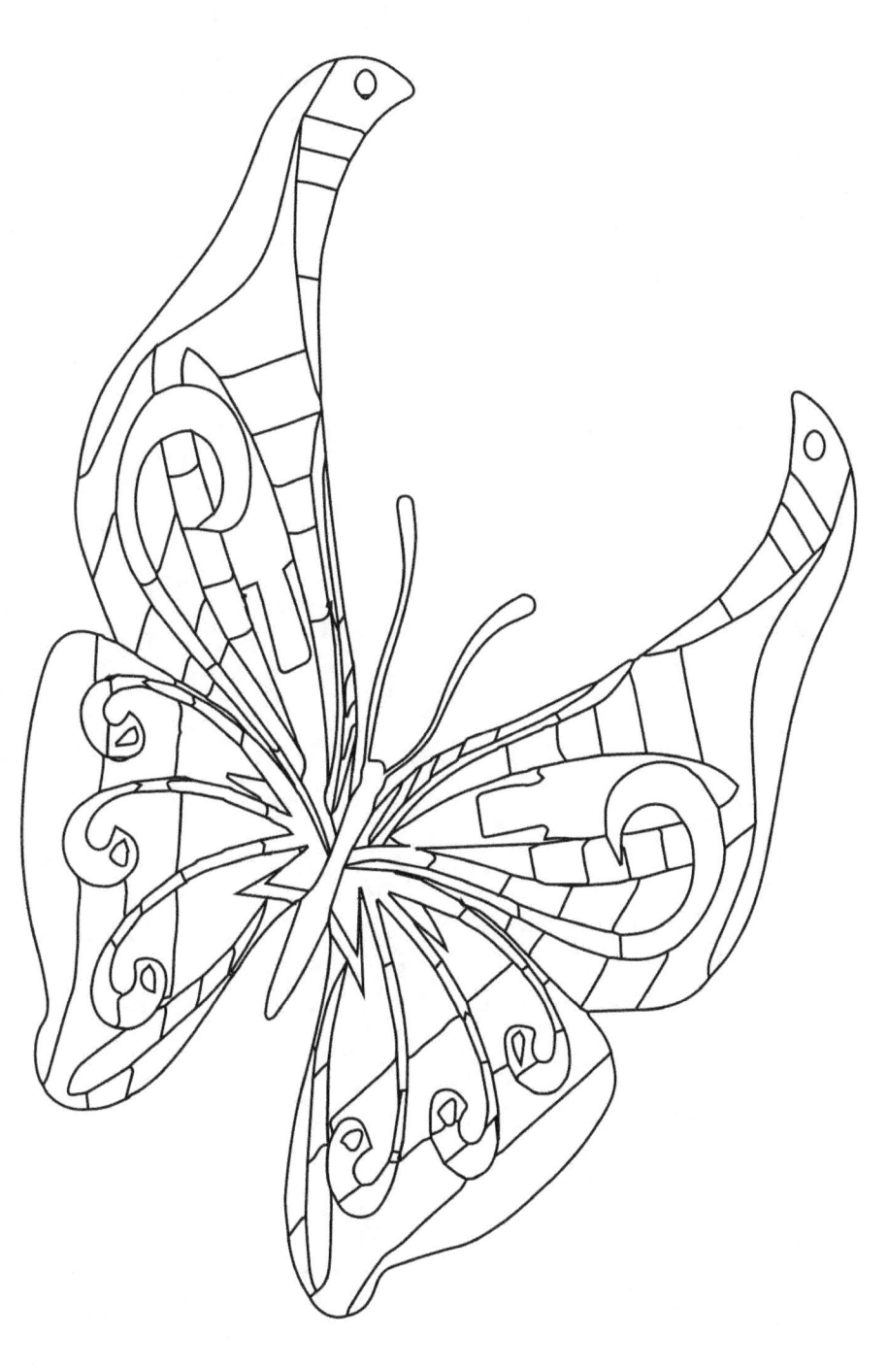

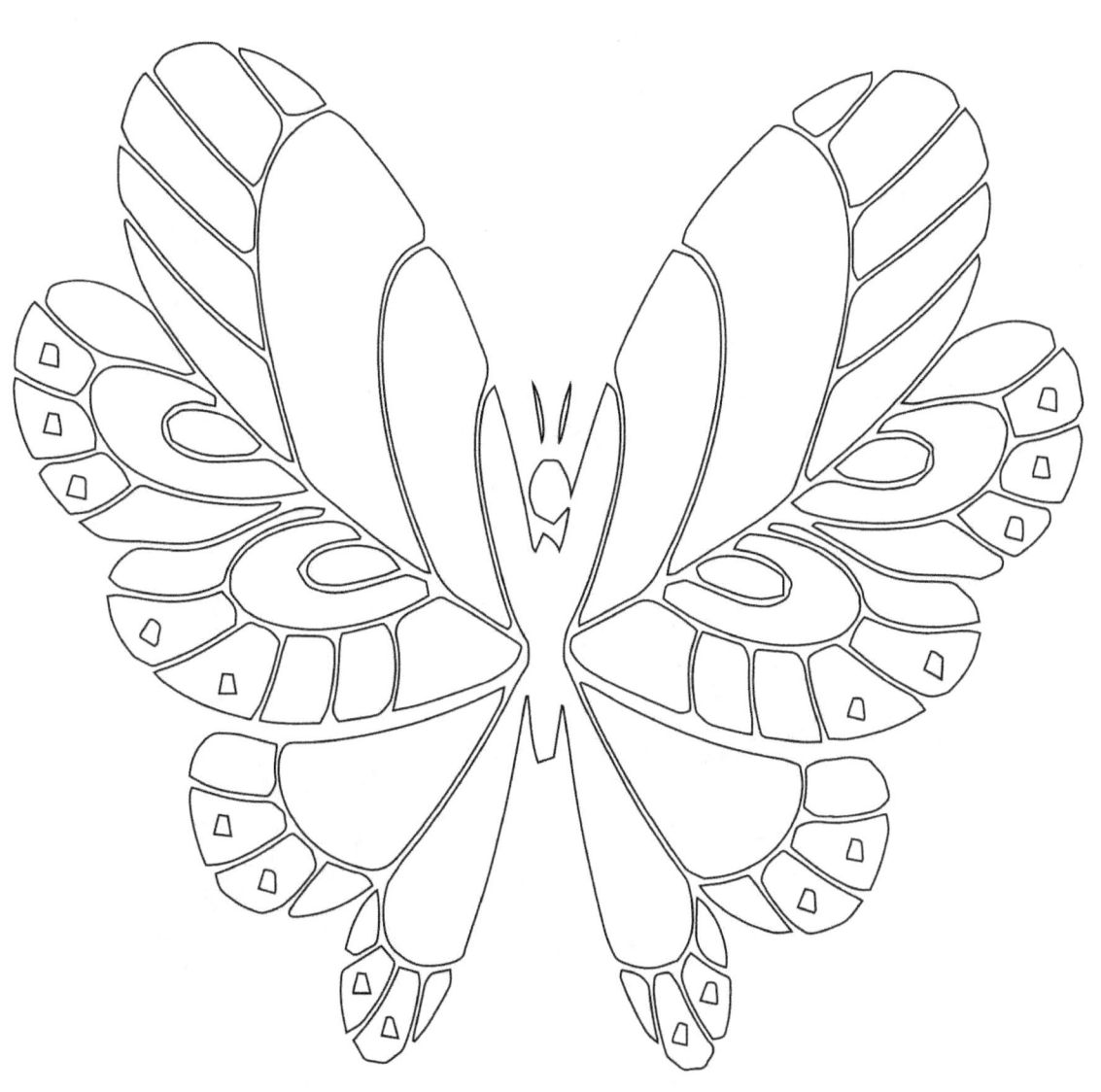

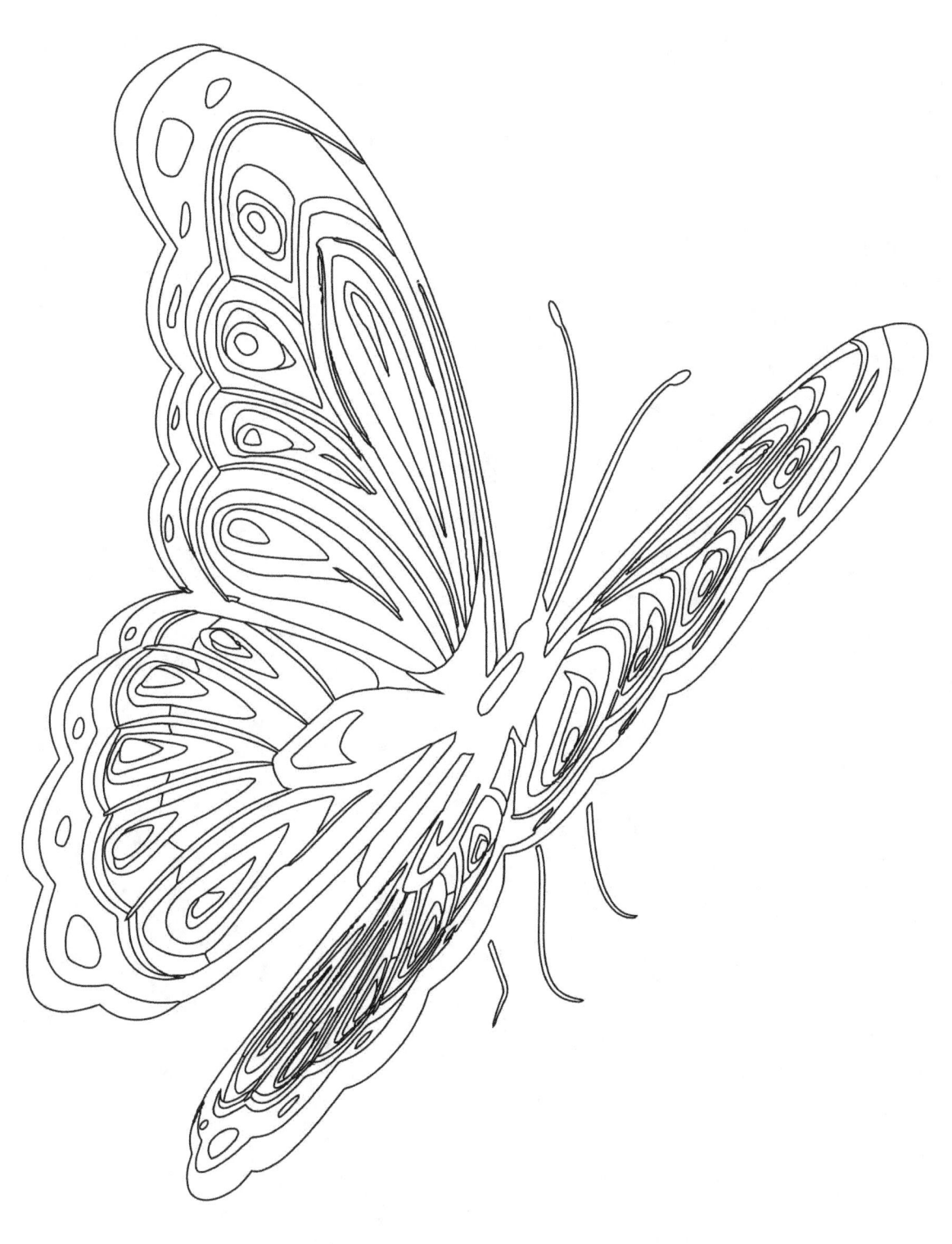

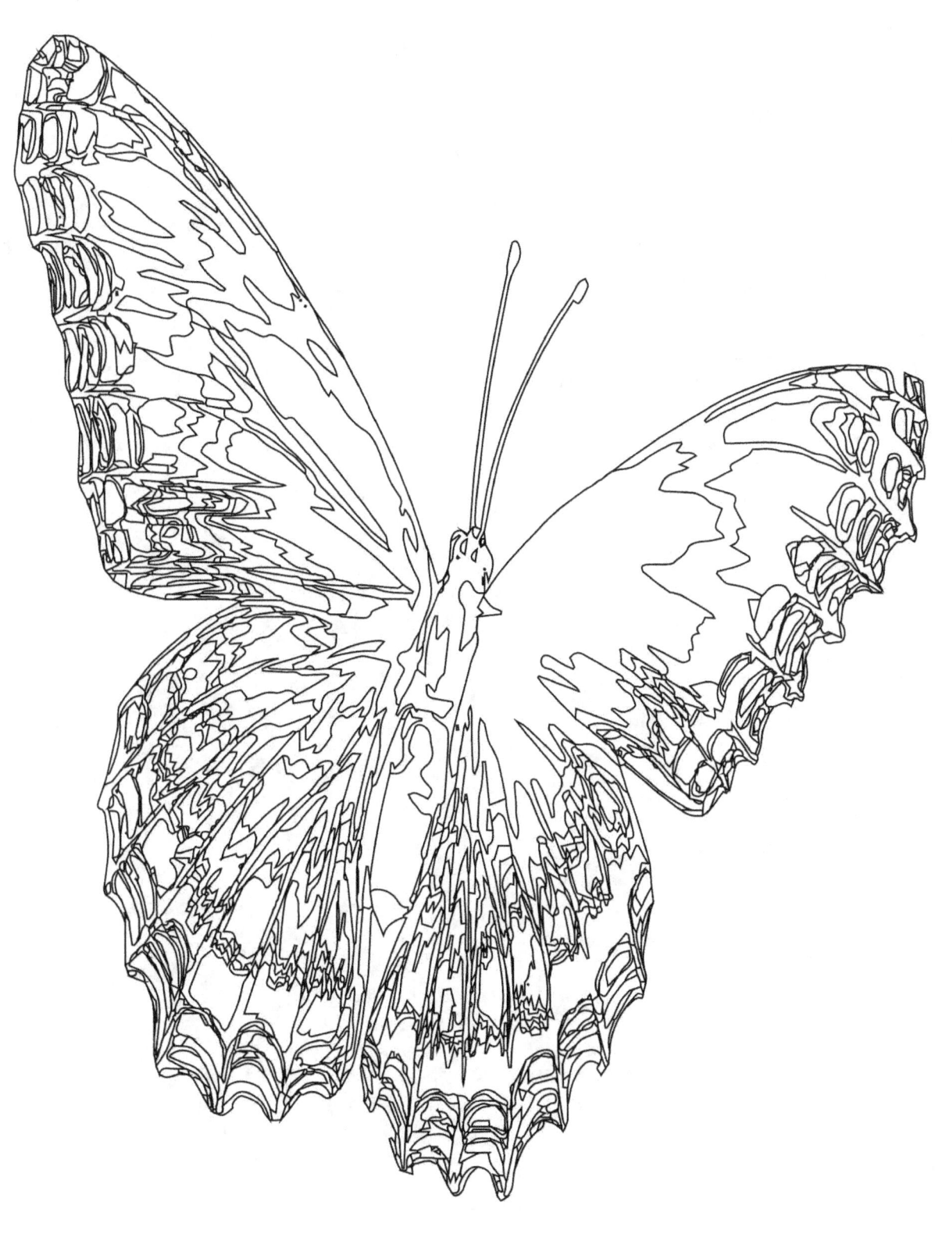

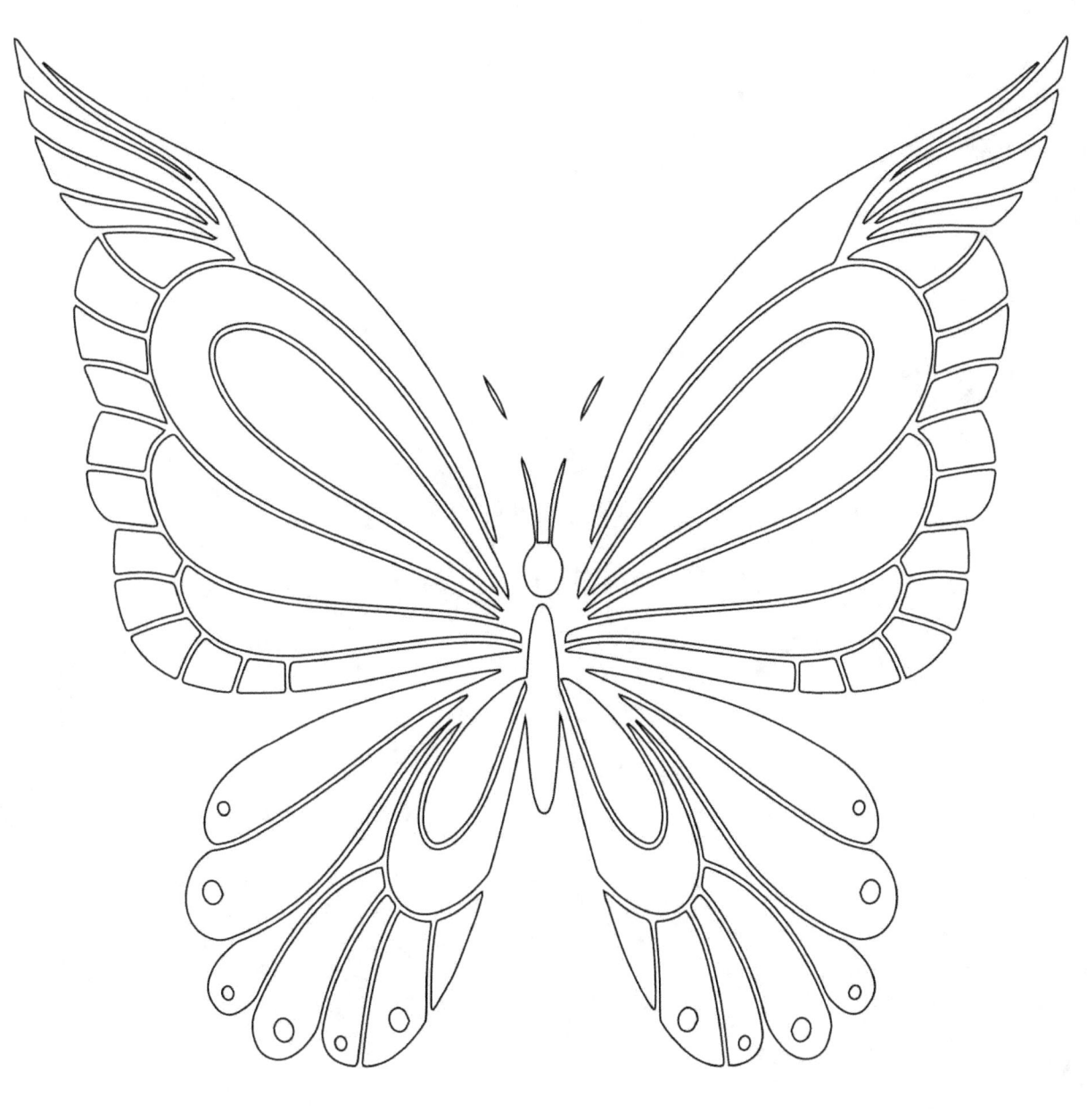

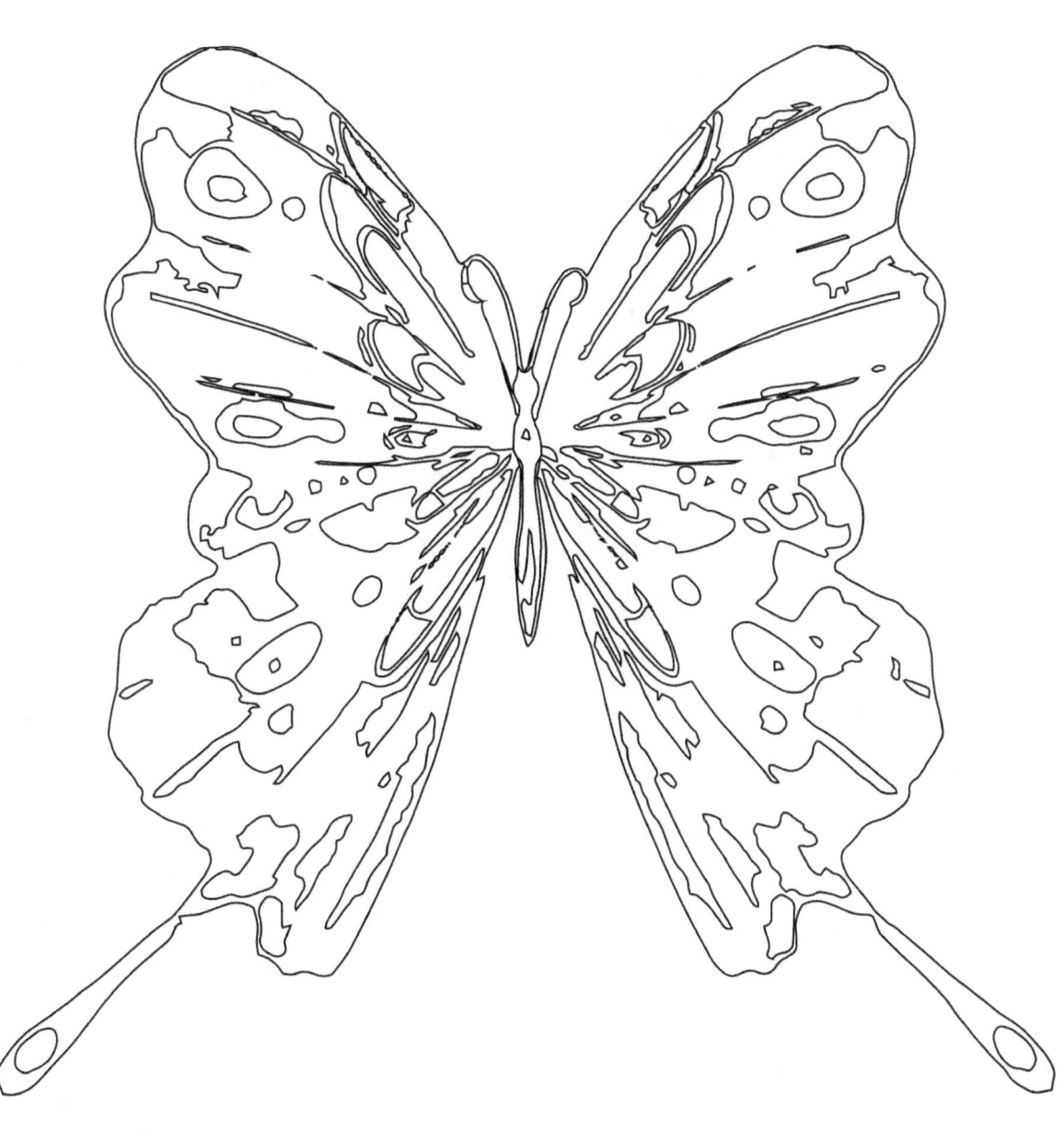

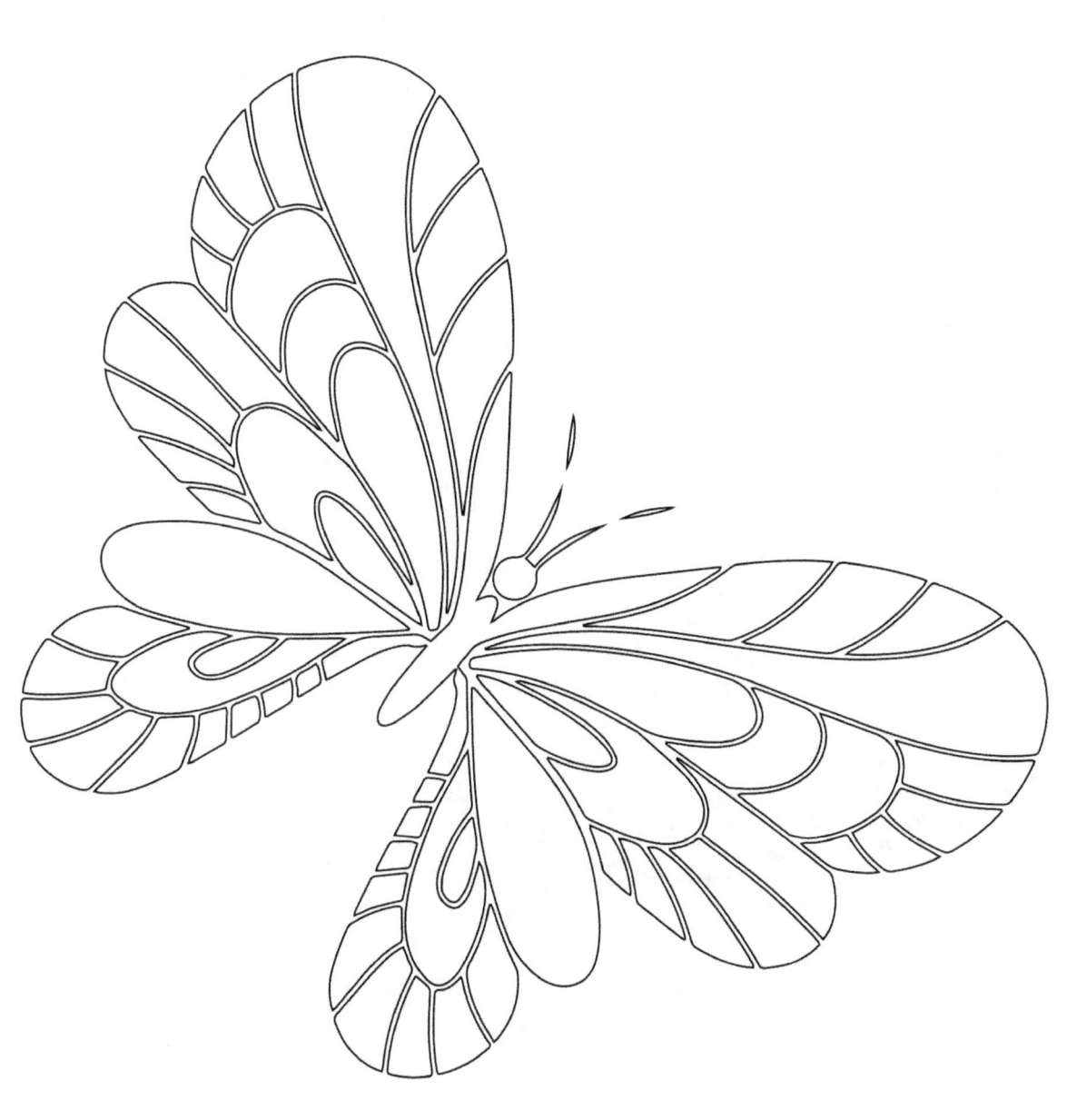

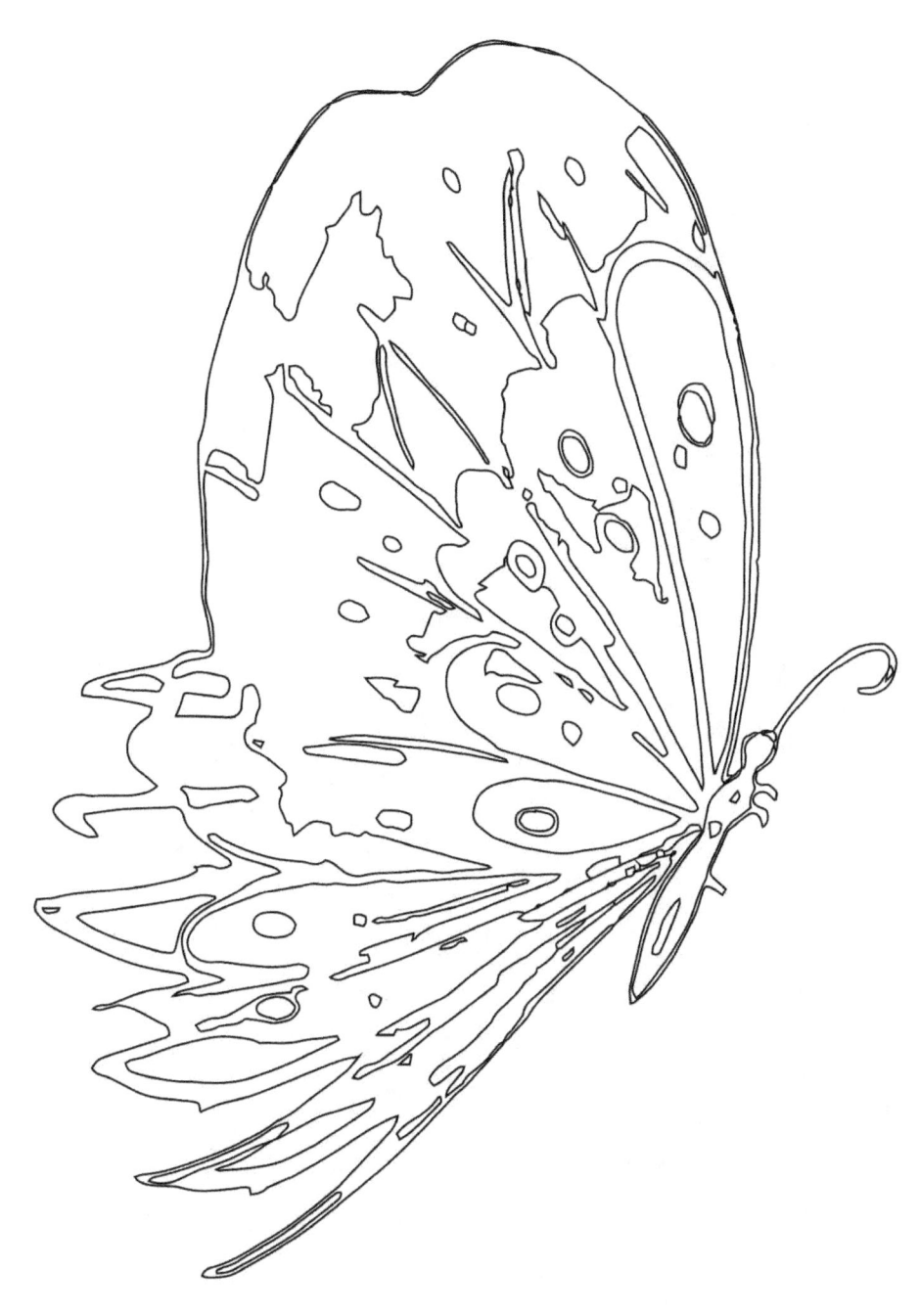

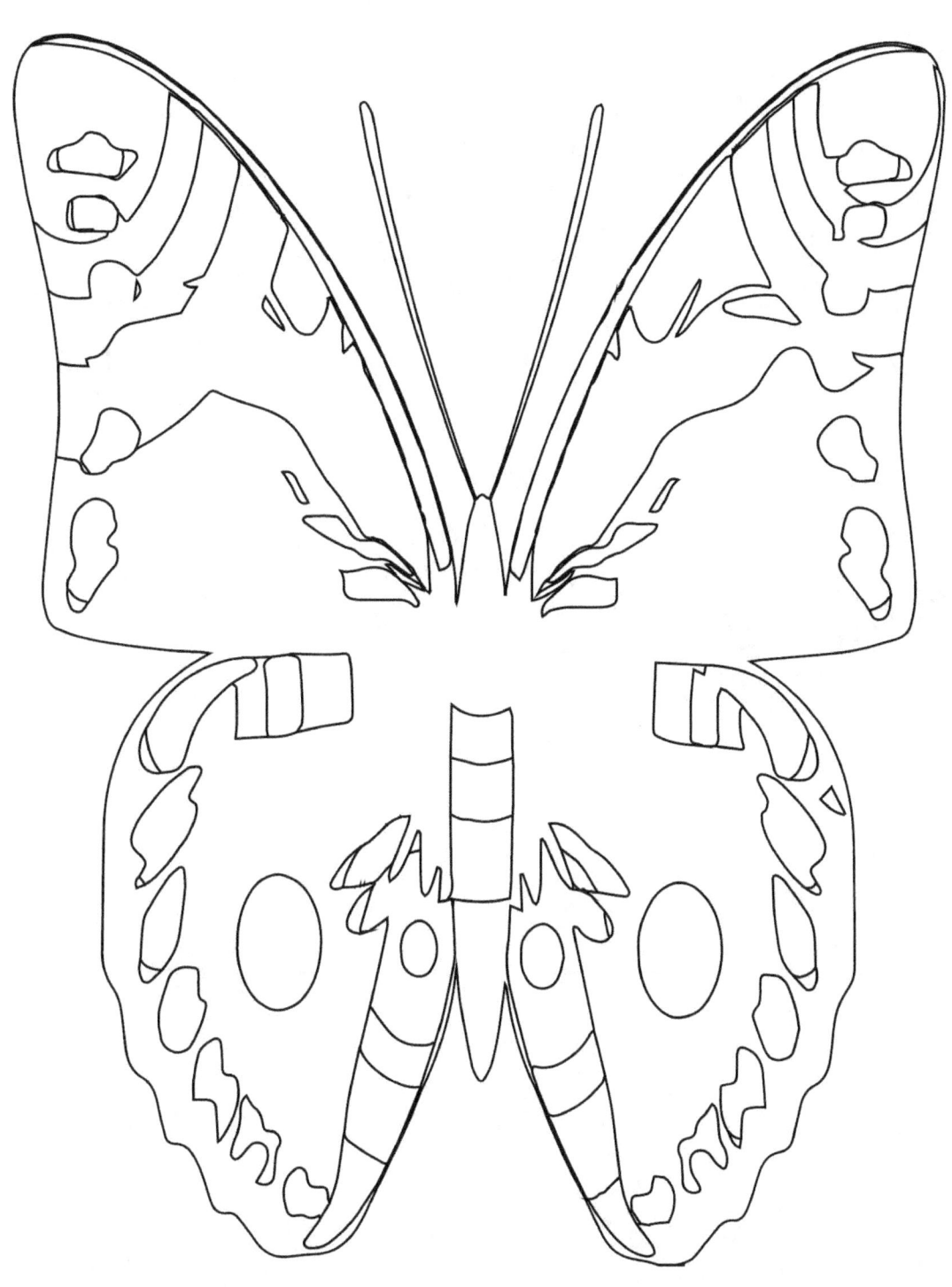

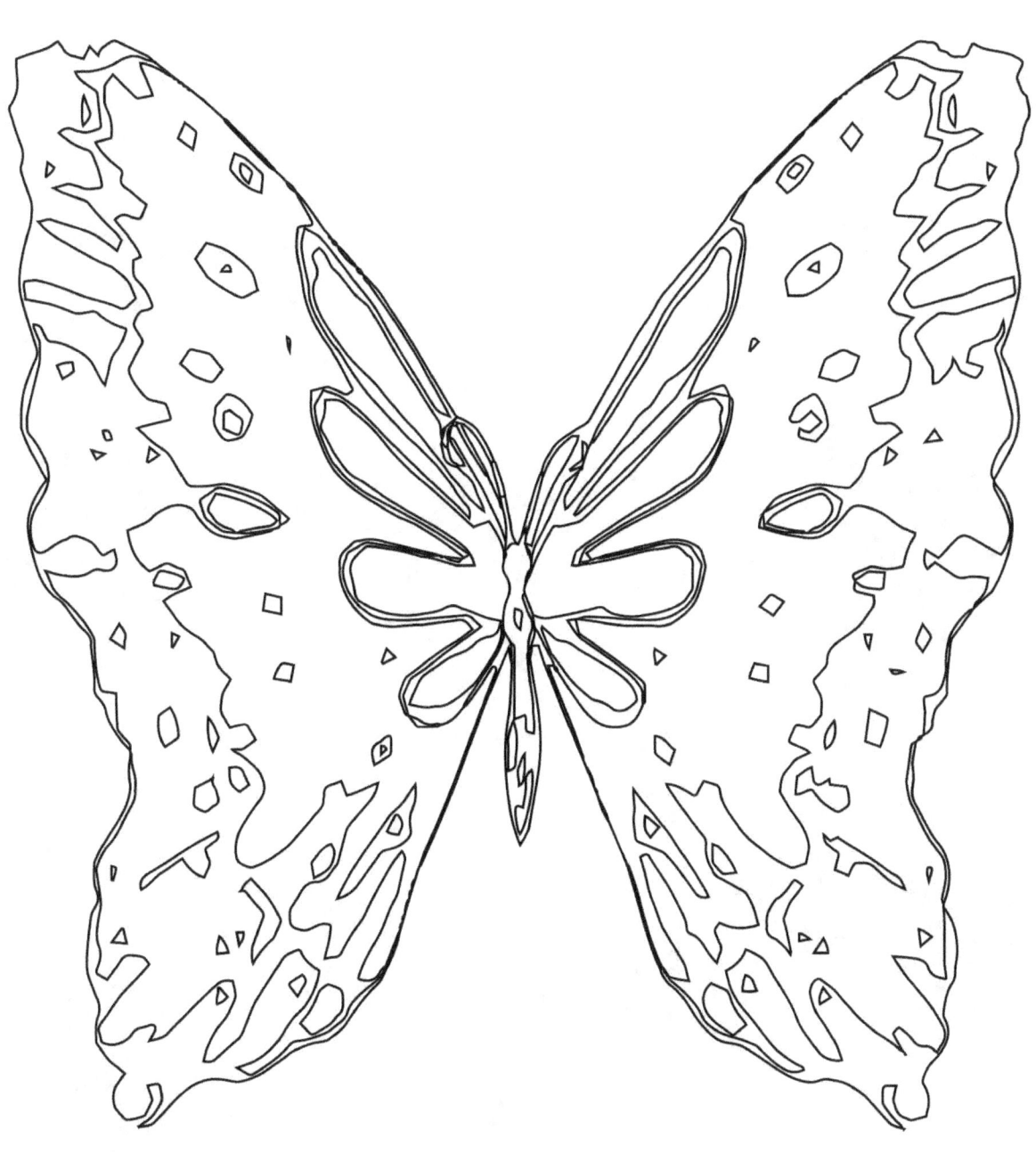

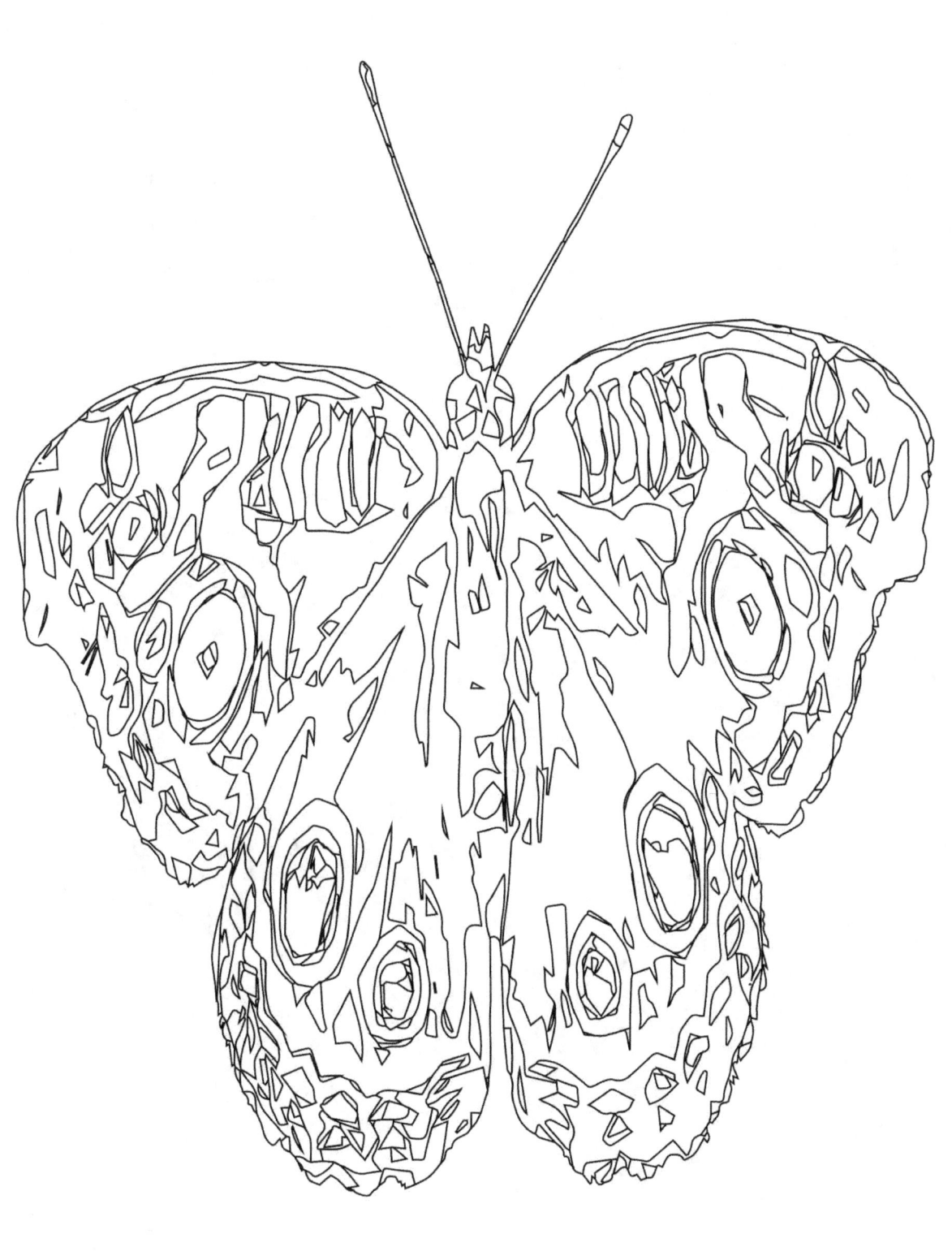

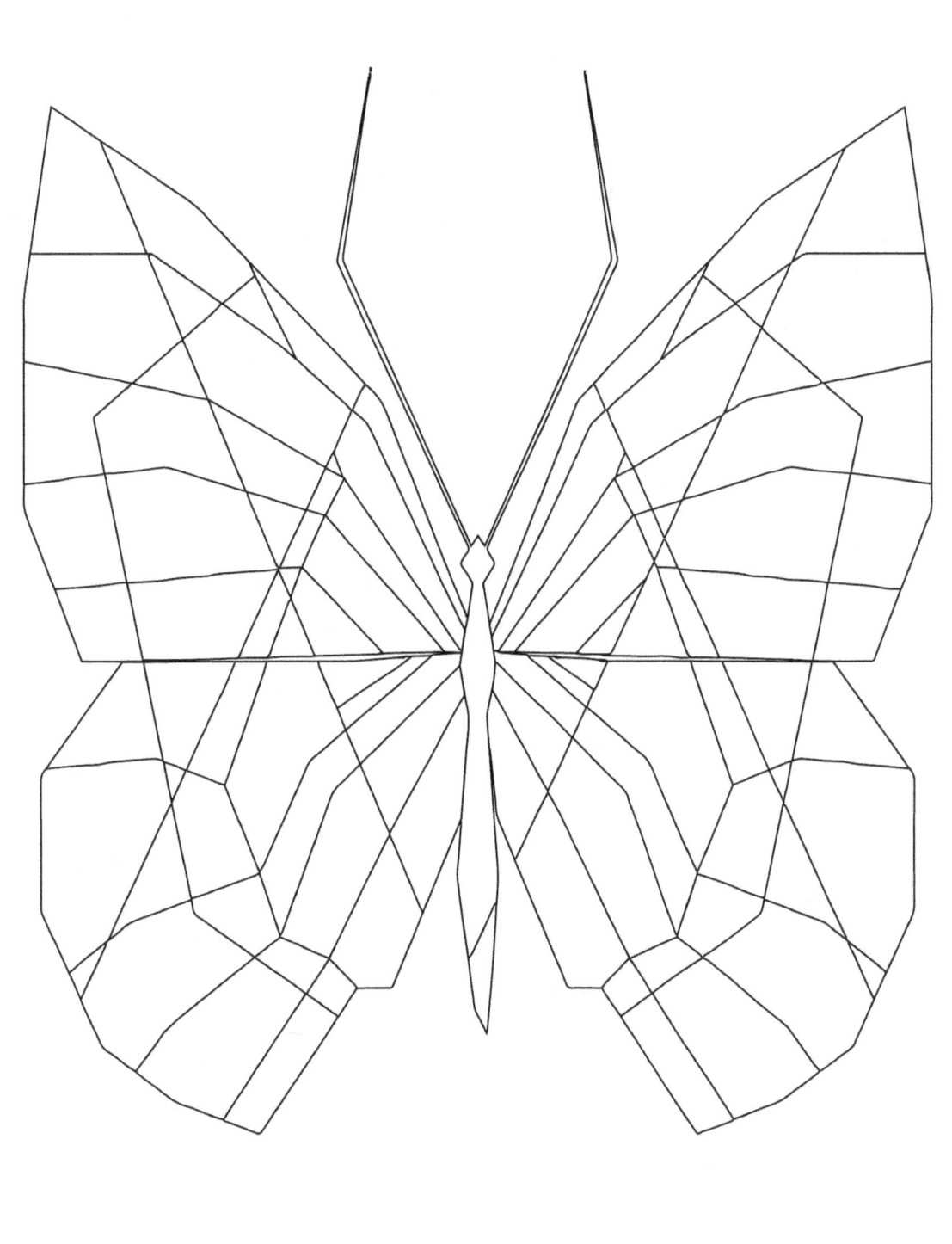

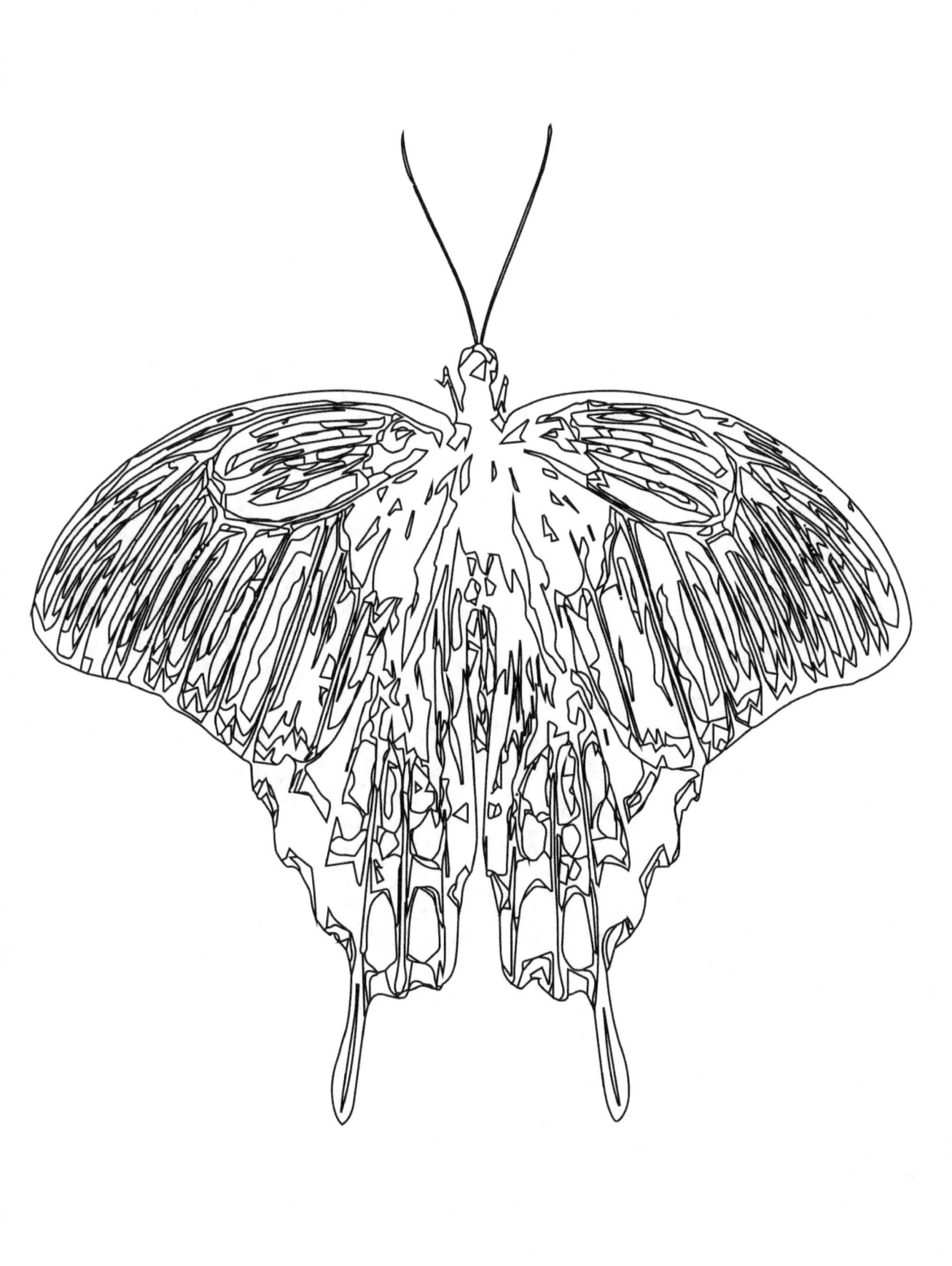

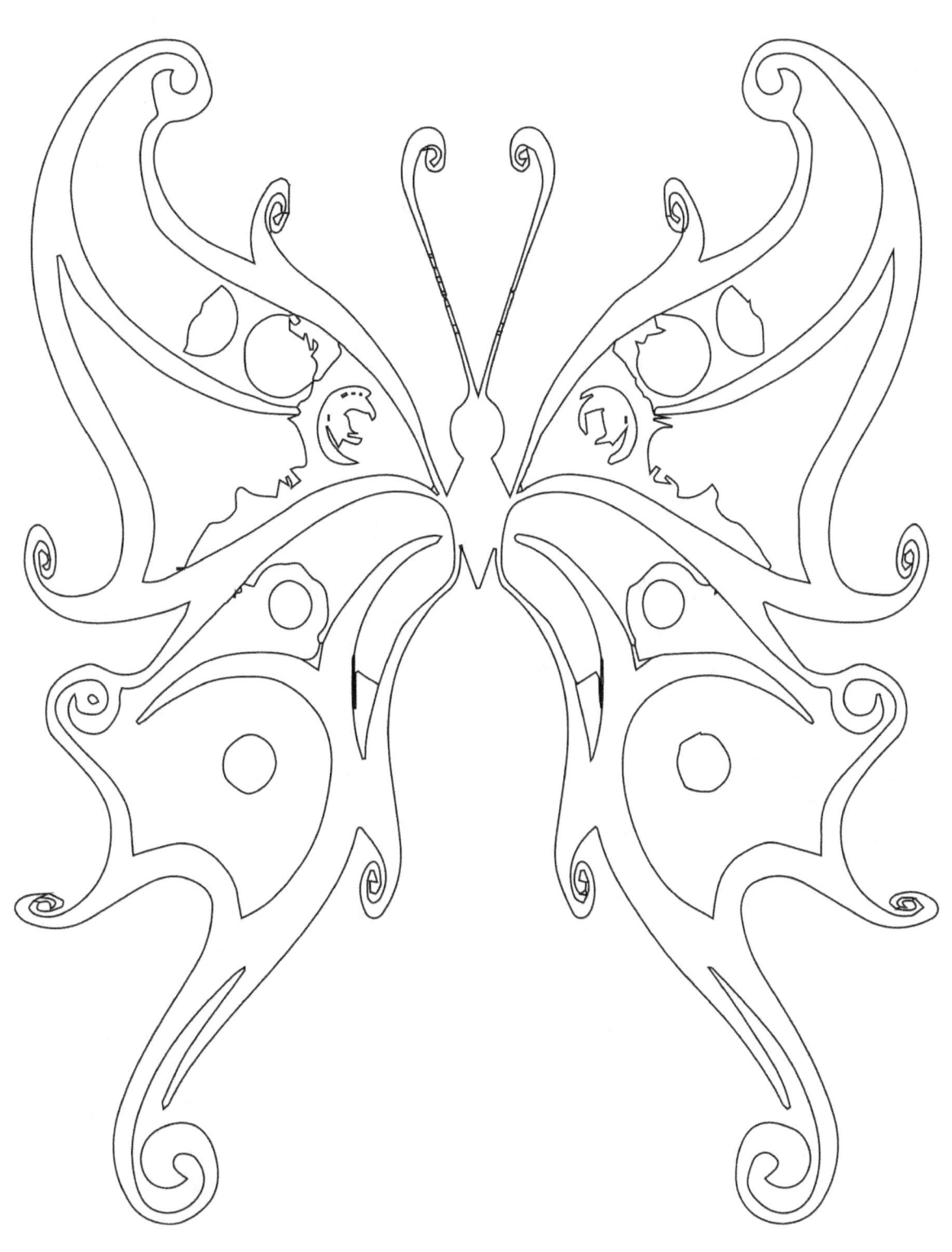

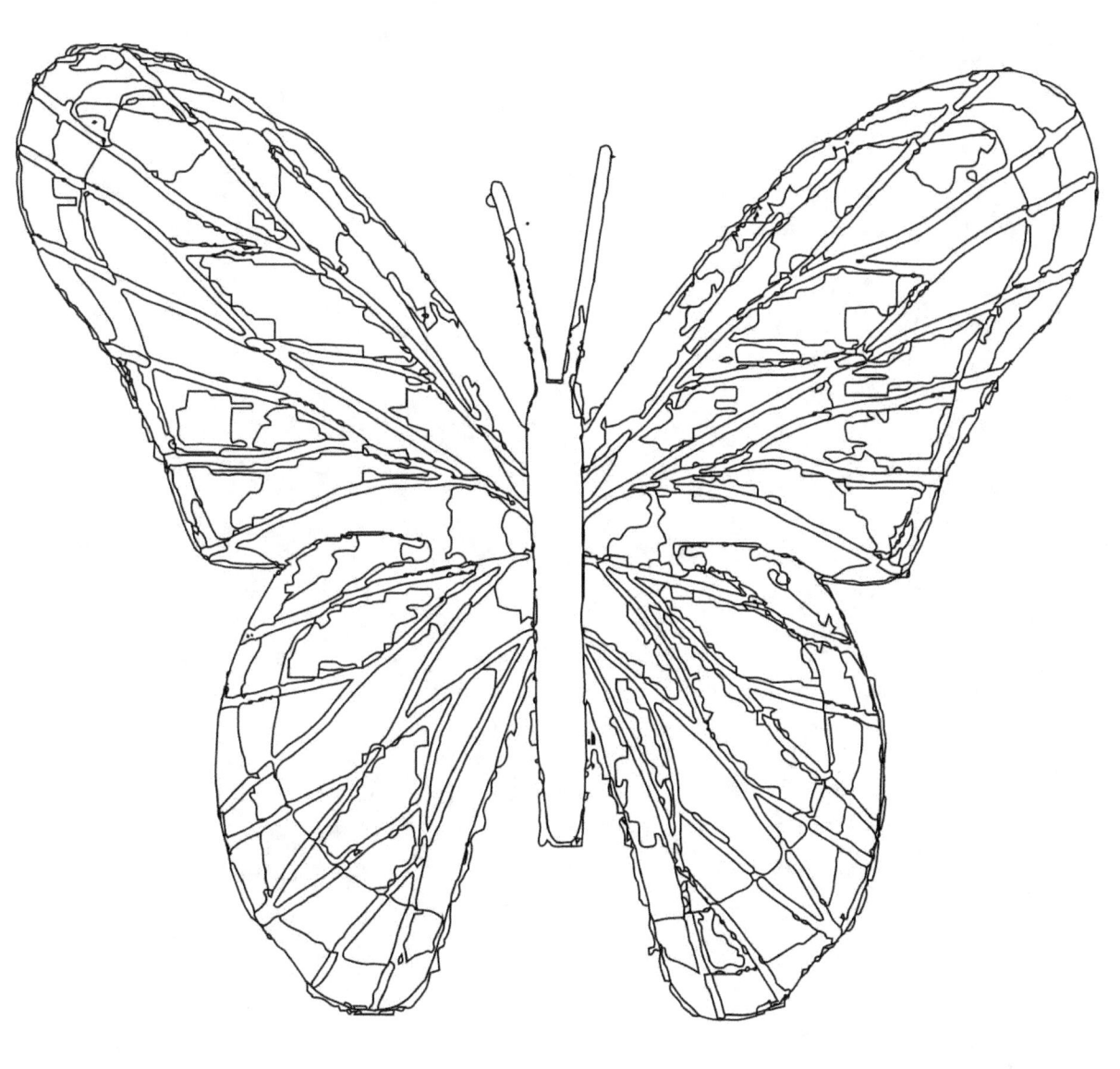

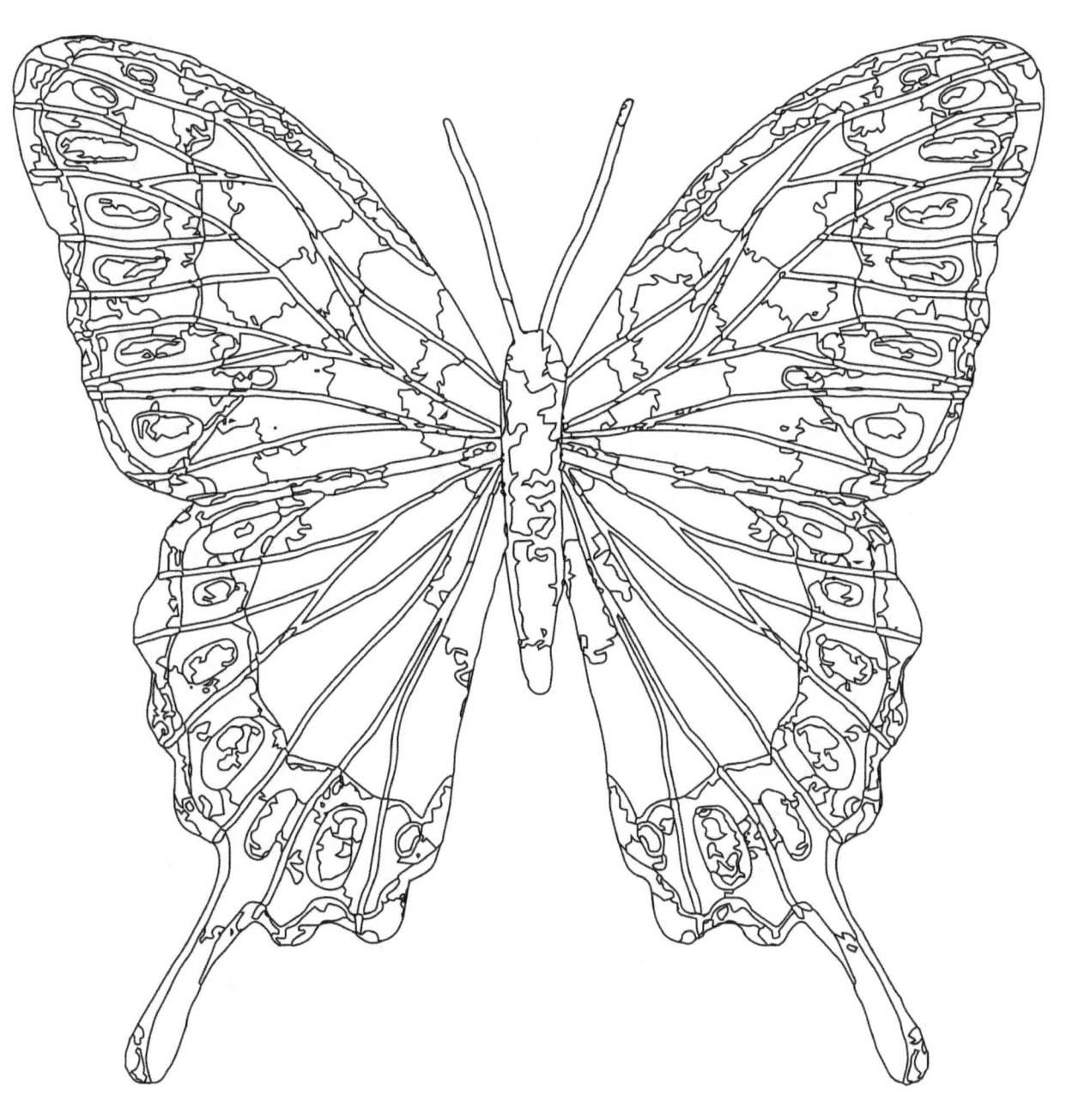

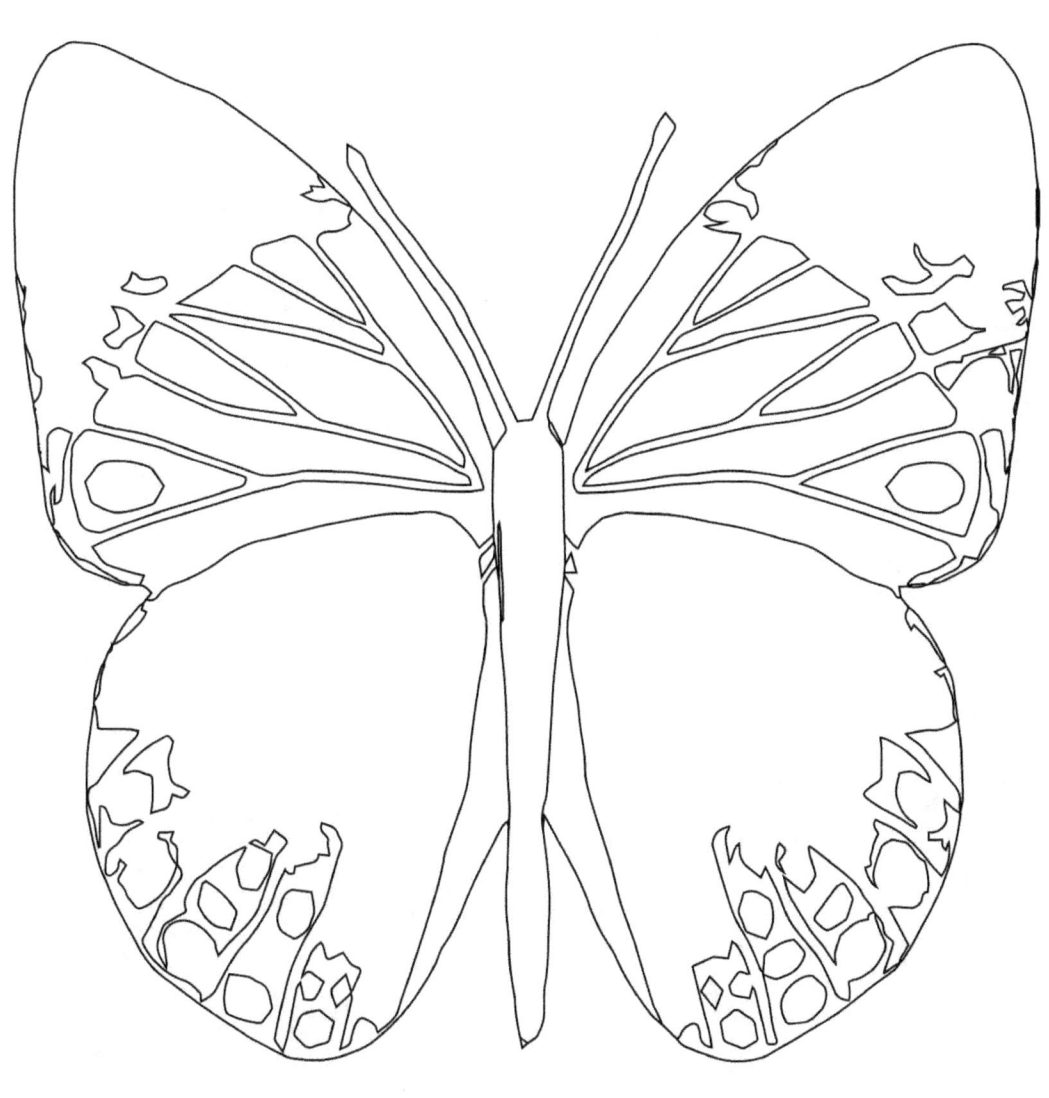

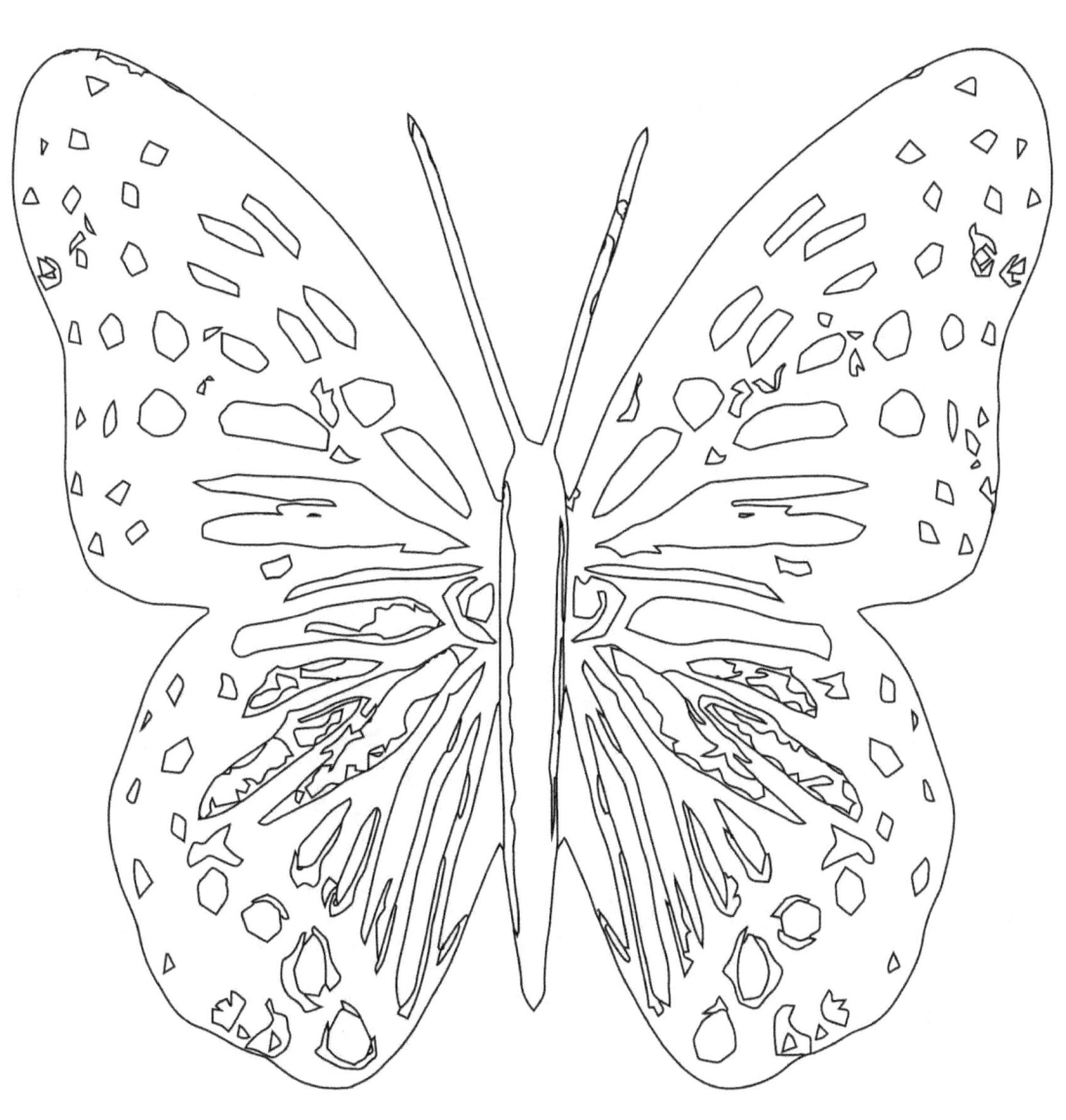

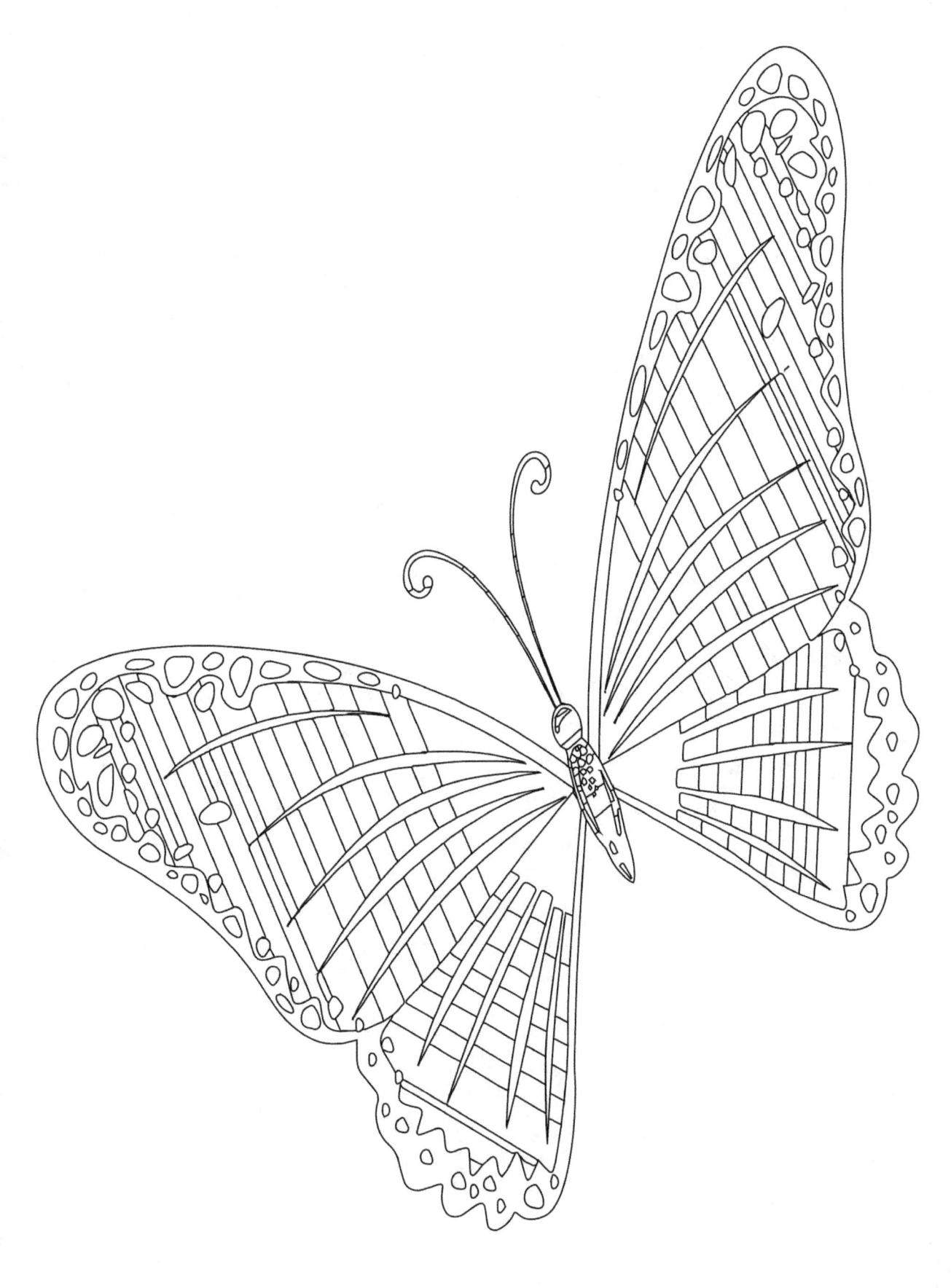

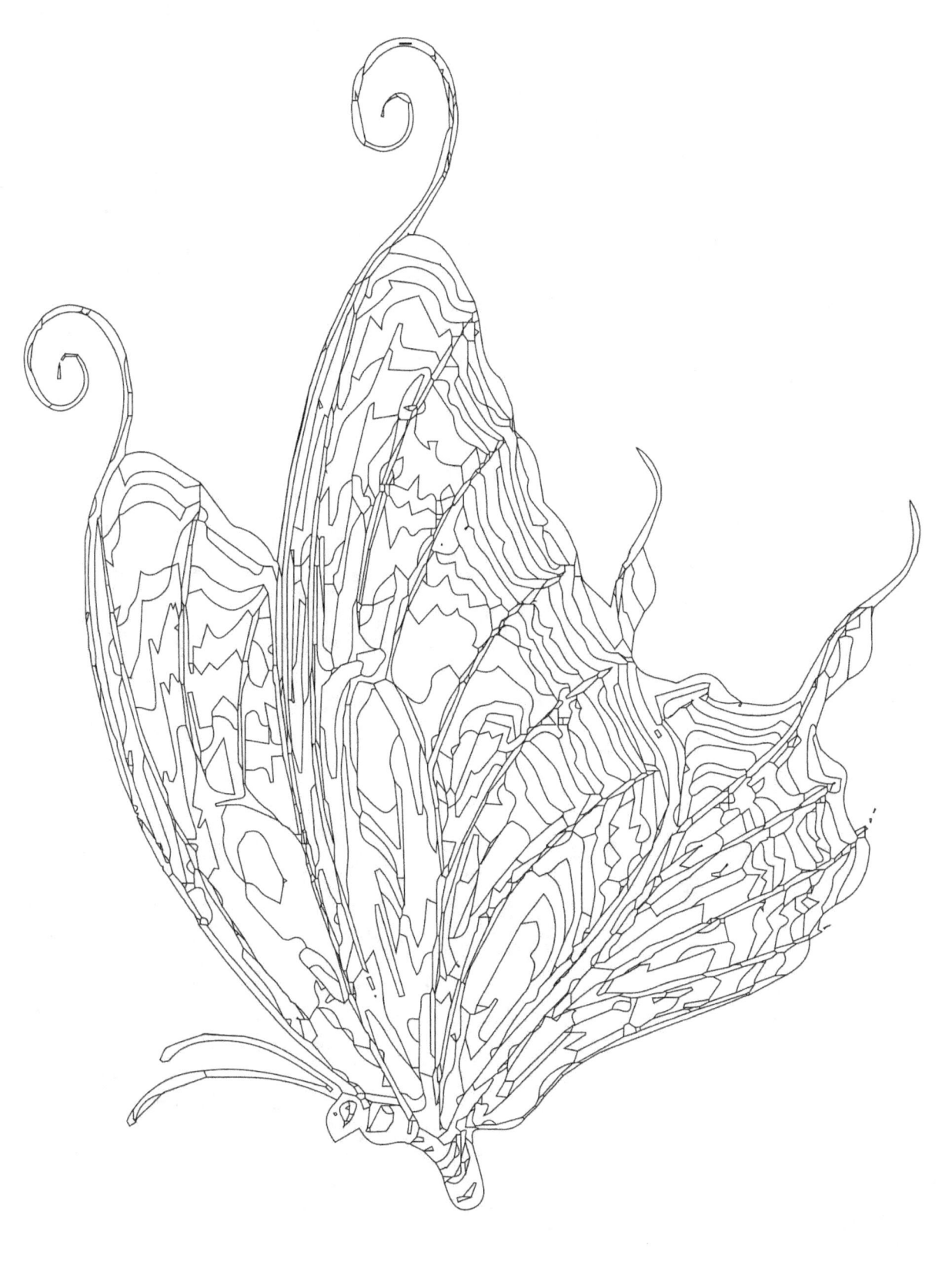

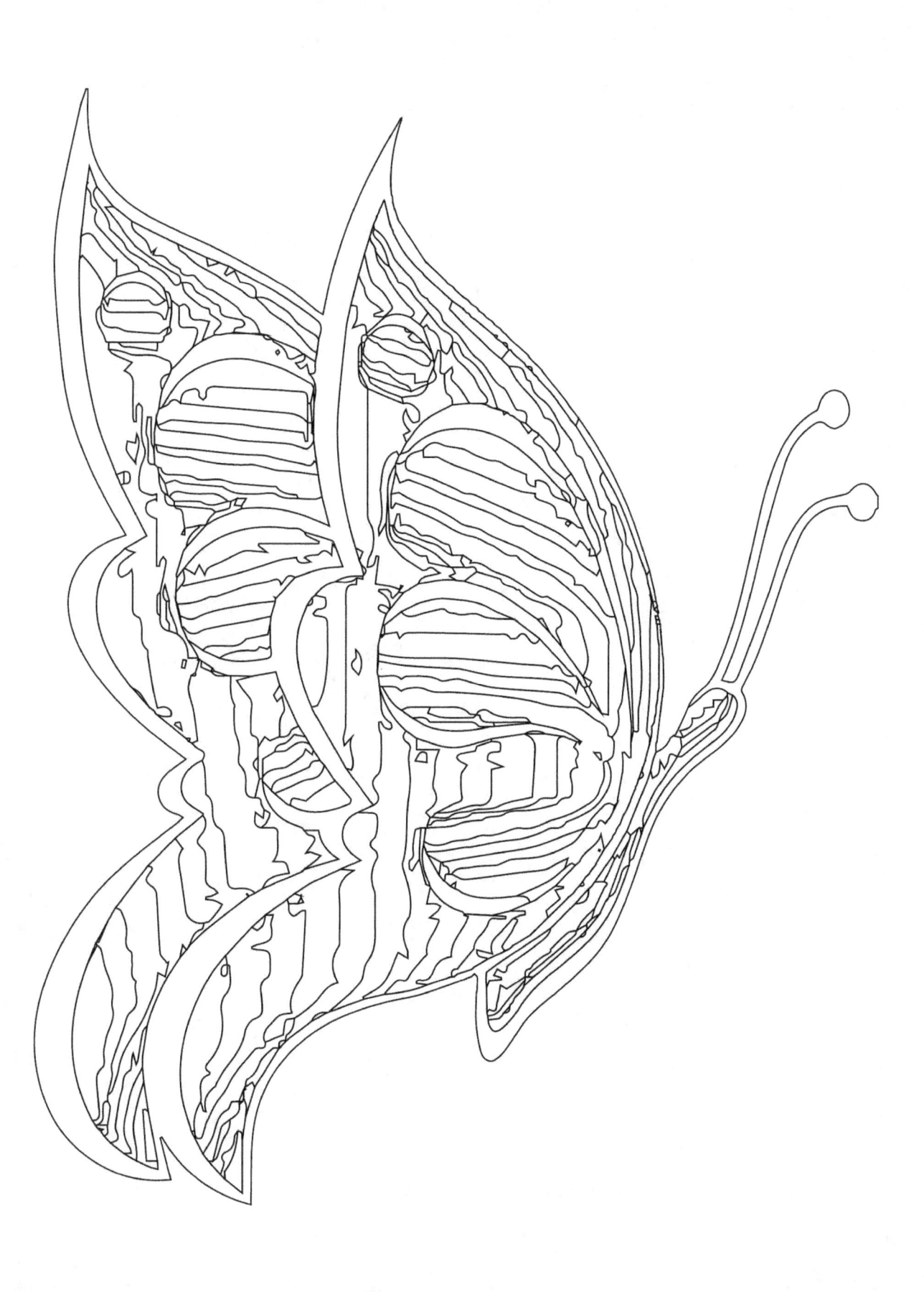

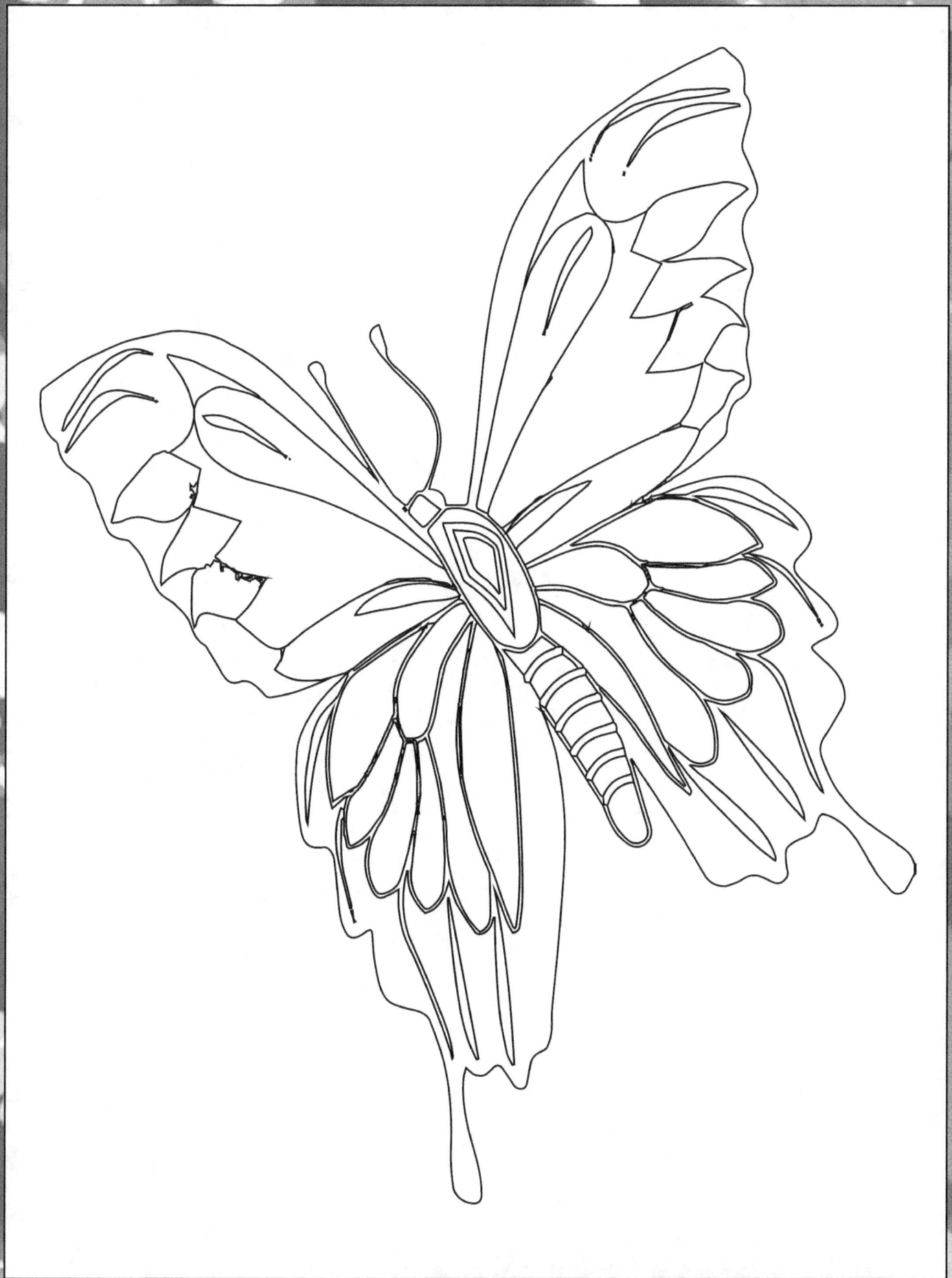

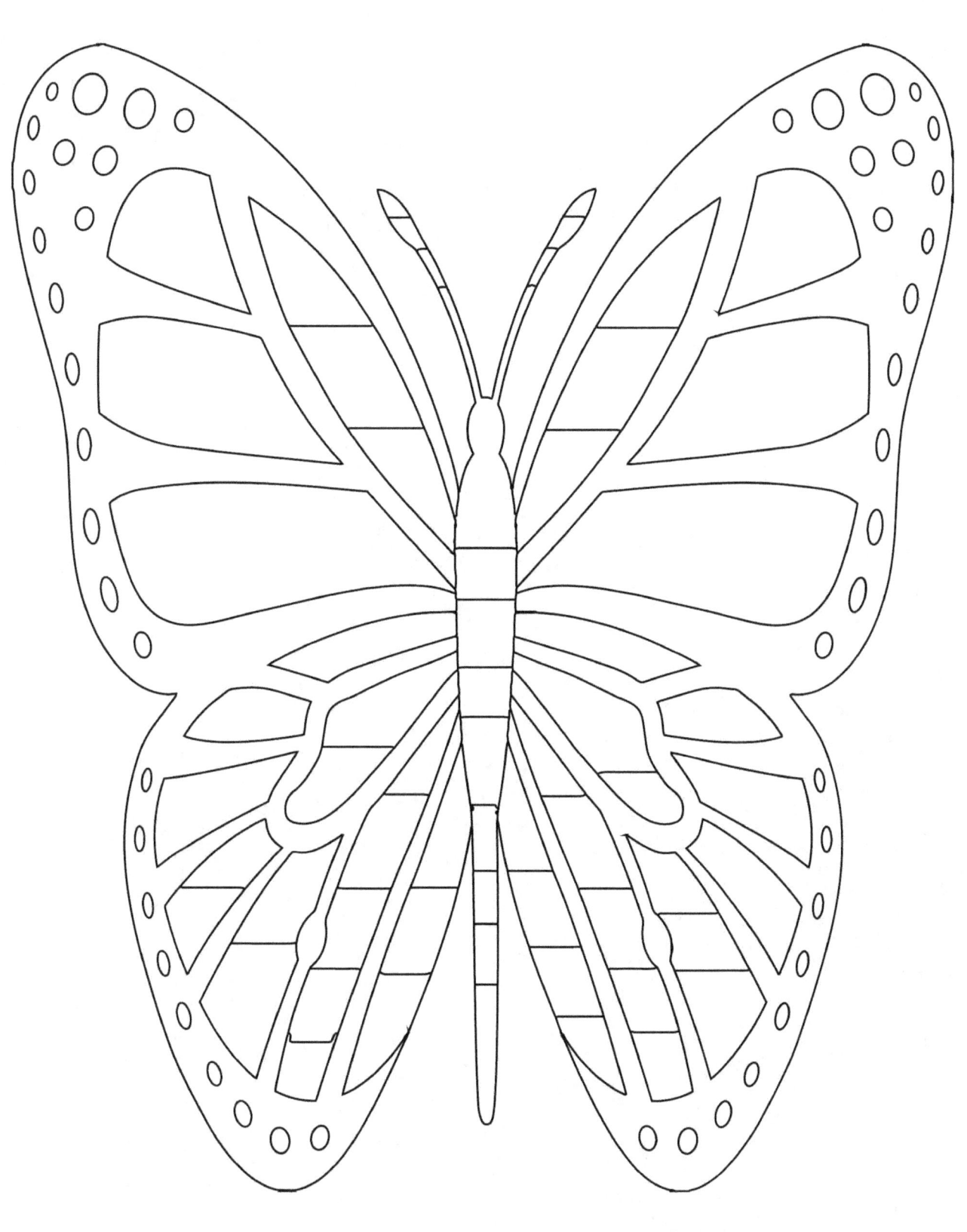

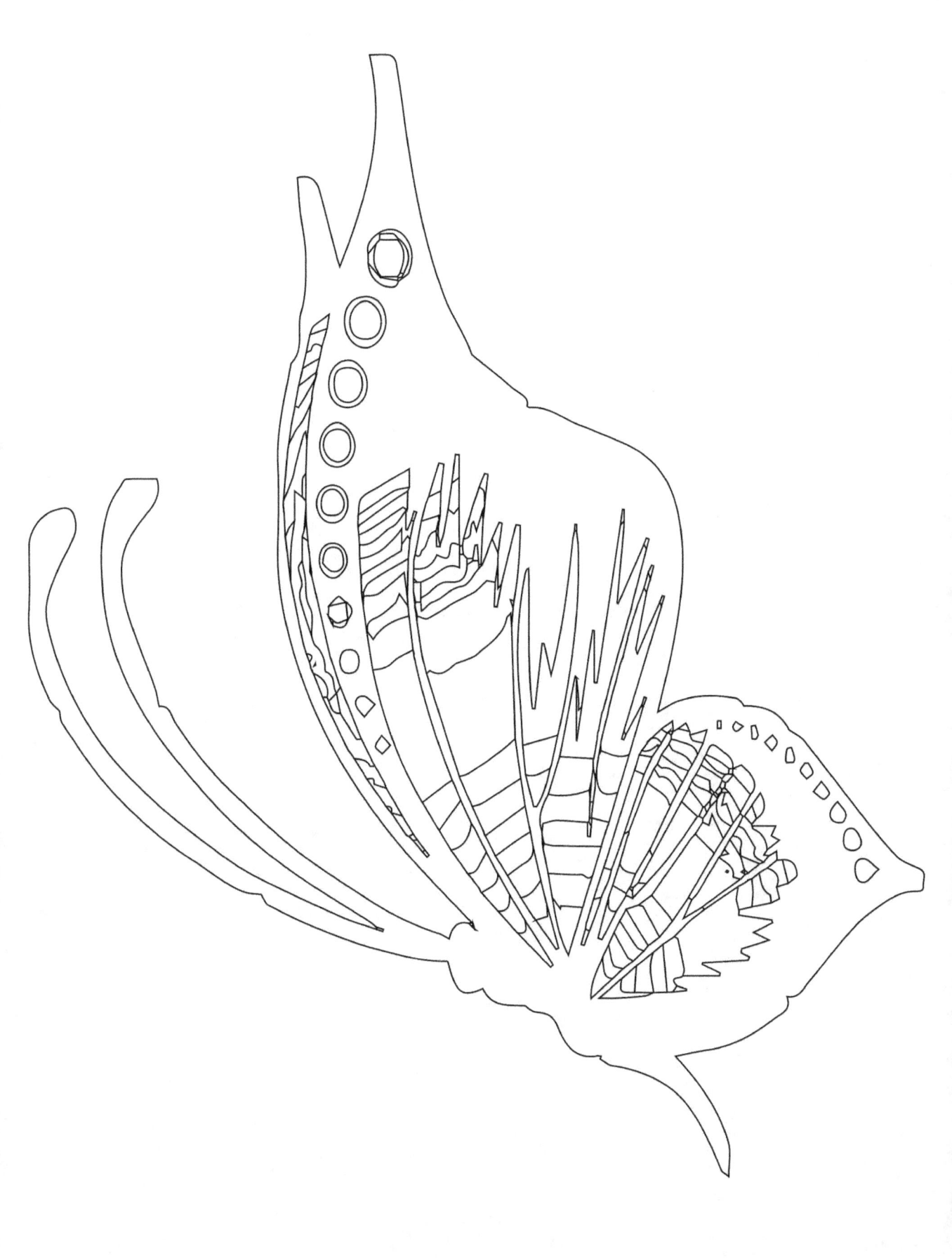

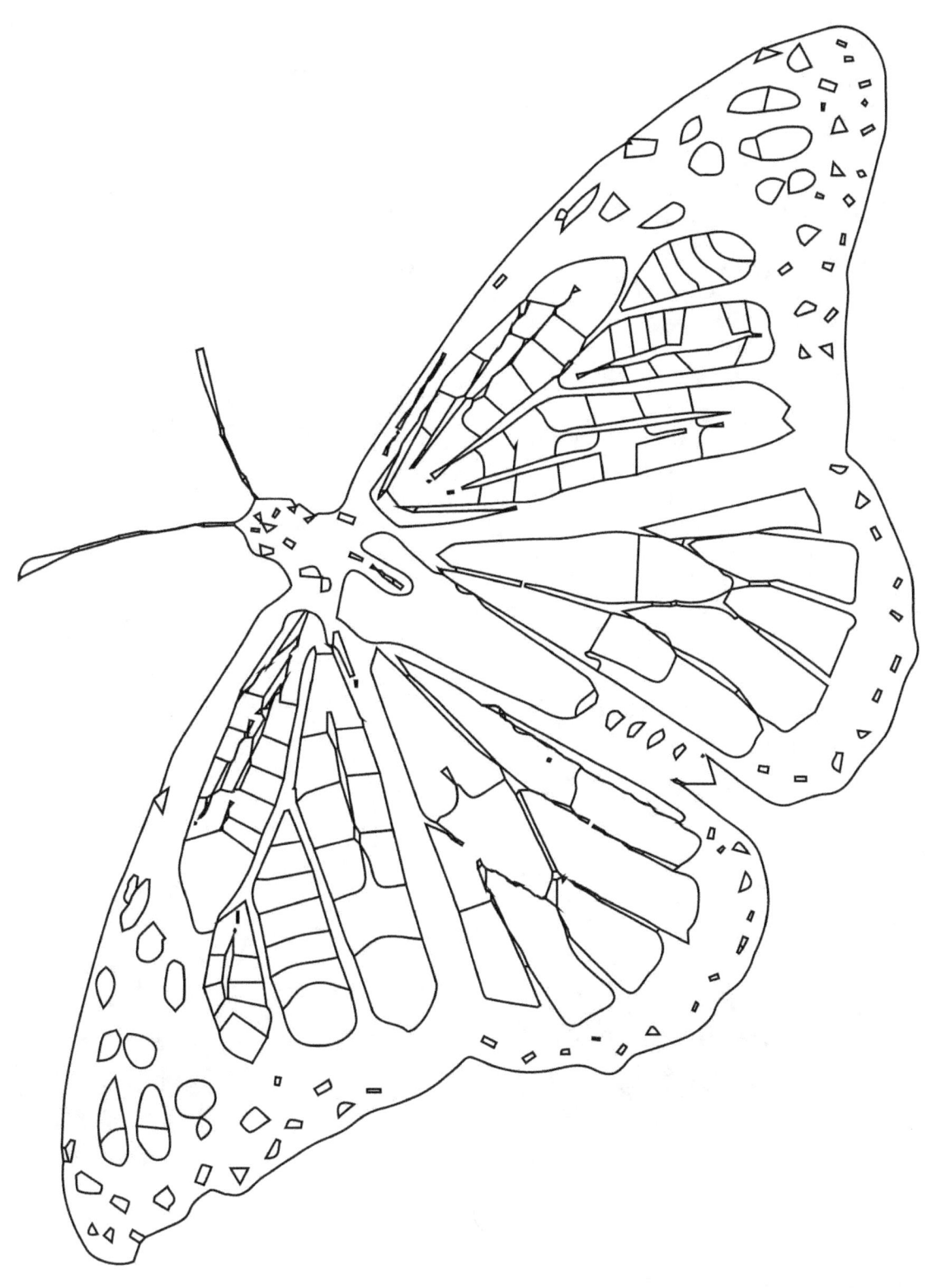

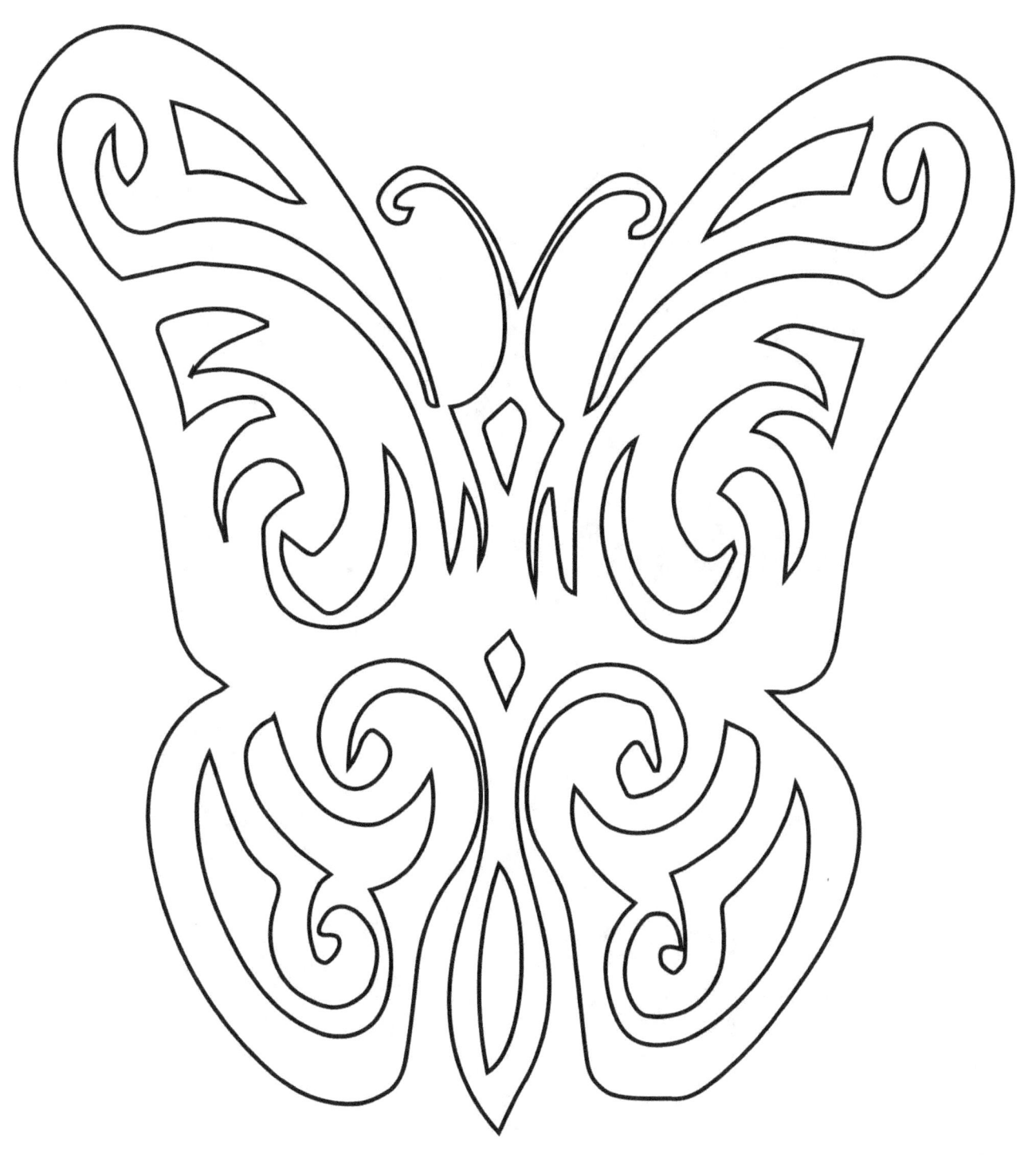

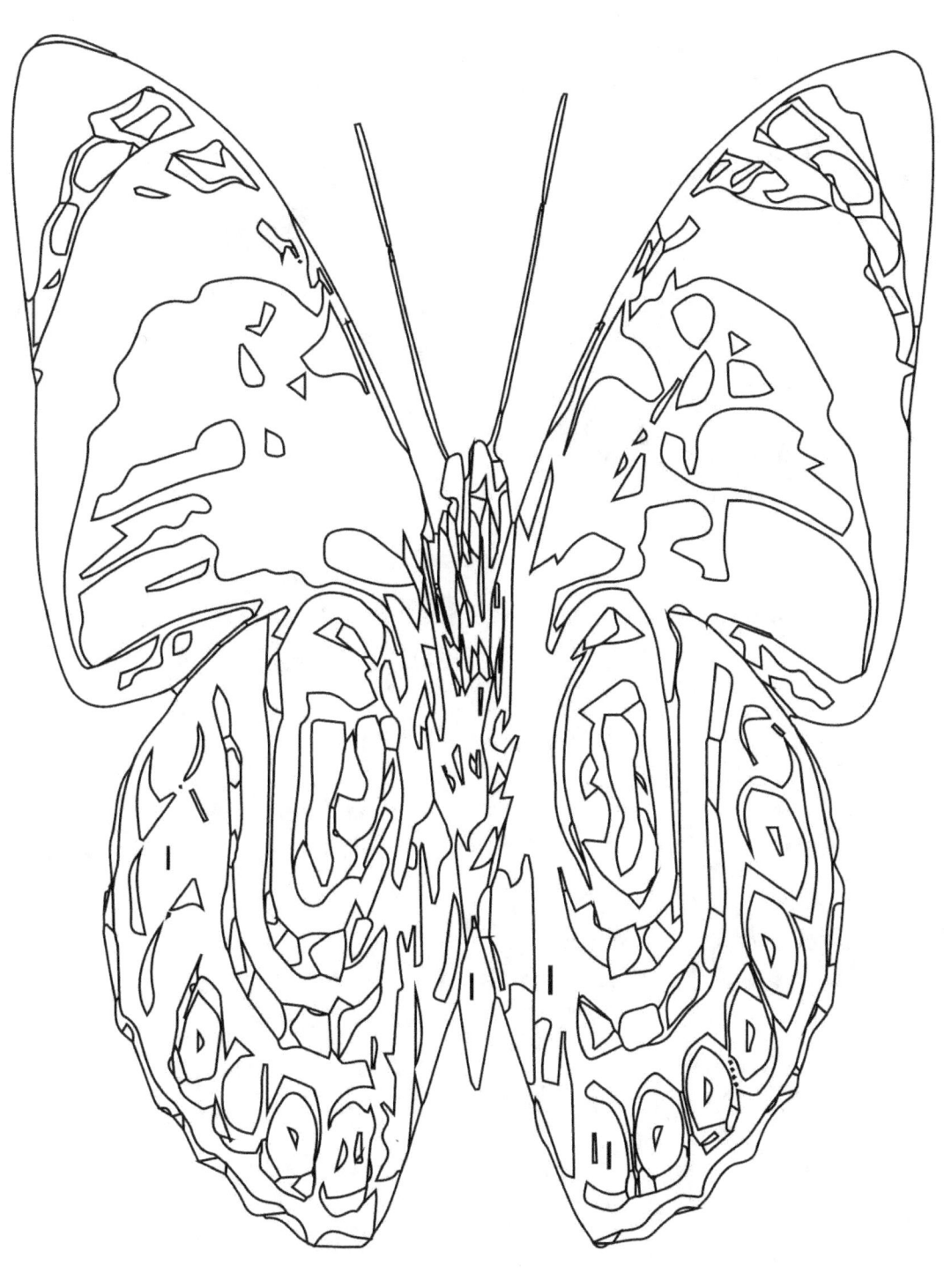